People in
Project Management

PEOPLE IN PROJECT MANAGEMENT

Edited by
J. Rodney Turner

GOWER

Published by
Gower Publishing Limited
Gower House
Croft Road
Aldershot
Hants GU11 3HR

Gower Publishing Company
Suite 420
101 Cherry Street
Burlington, VT 05401-4405 USA

British Library Cataloguing in Publication Data

People in project management
  1. Project management 2. Personnel management
  I. Turner, Rodney
  658.4'04

ISBN 0 566 08530 5

Library of Congress Cataloging-in-Publication Data

People in project management / edited by J. Rodney Turner.
      p. cm.
"This book is derived from the Gower handbook of project management, 3rd edition"--Pref.
Includes bibliographical references.
ISBN 0-566-08530-5
1. Project management. 2. Personnel management. I. Turner, J. Rodney (John Rodney), 1953– II. Gower handbook of project management.

HD69.P75 P4627 2003
658.4'04--dc21

2002032523

Typeset in 10 point Century Old Style by Bournemouth Colour Press, Parkstone and printed in Great Britain by MPG Books Limited, Bodmin, Cornwall

Contents

List of figures ix
Notes on contributors xi
Preface xv

1 **Managing human resources in the project-based organization** 1
Anne Keegan and Rodney Turner

From operation to projects 2
Selection in the project-based firm 3
Career development for a changing environment 5
Continuity and change in people management 8
Conclusions 10
References and further reading 11

2 **Assessing and developing the project management competence of individuals** 13
Lynn Crawford

Approaches to defining competence 14
Standards for assessment and development of project management competence 19
The role of assessment and development of project management competence 22
Corporate approaches to assessing and developing project management competence 24
Conclusions 27
References and further reading 28

3 **Project management competences in the project-oriented
   organization**   **31**
   Roland Gareis and Martina Huemann

   Strategy, structure and culture of the project-oriented organization   31
   Project management as a business process of the project-oriented
   organization   33
   Project management competences of individuals and project teams   34
   Project management competences of organizations   36
   The project management competence model   36
   Benchmarking organizational project management competences   40
   Further development of organizational project management
   competences   41
   Specific management competences in the project-oriented
   organization   42
   References and further reading   42

4 **Delivering improved project management maturity through
   experiential learning**   **45**
   Rodney Turner, Anne Keegan and Lynn Crawford

   Experiential learning in project management competence
   development   46
   Experiential learning of individuals   50
   Experiential learning in project-based organizations   55
   Conclusions   61
   References and further reading   62

5 **Managing teams: the reality of life**   **65**
   Tony Reid

   Results through teamworking   66
   Practical guidelines   66
   Further opportunities for growth   74
   References and further reading   81

6 **Managing and leading**   **83**
   David Partington

   Theories of leadership   85
   The trait approach   86
   The behavioural approach   88

The contingency approach 90
The visionary approach 93
Conclusions 96
References and further reading 97

7 Managing stakeholders **99**
Bill McElroy and Chris Mills

Definitions 99
The stakeholder management process 103
Hints and tips 116
Acknowledgement 117
Reference and further reading 117

8 Managing conflict, persuasion and negotiation **119**
Bob Graham

Avoiding conflict 120
Developing an influence strategy 121
Resolving conflict 128
The power and value of information 130
Conclusions 133
References and further reading 133

9 Managing culture **135**
David Rees

Definitions of culture 136
Culture in business 137
Impact of culture on performance 140
Managing culture in projects 141
Managing cultural integration 144
Managing international cultures 147
Paradigm shift 150
Conclusions 156
References and further reading 156

10 Managing ethics **159**
Alistair Godbold

Ethics and project management 160
Ethics as a differentiator 164
Ethical theory 164

Ethics abroad   168
Practical help   169
Conclusions   170
References and further reading   171

Index   173

List of figures

2.1   Integrated model of competence identifying key components of
       competences   18
2.2   Knowledge-based project management standards, assessment
       processes and qualifications   21
2.3   Project management professional and government-recognized
       qualifications in Australia   22
2.4   A model for assessment and development of workplace
       competence   23
2.5   Process for project management development   26
3.1   Strategy, structure and culture of the project-oriented
       organization   32
3.2   Role description 'Project Manager'   35
3.3   Maturity levels of the SEI Capability Maturity Model   37
3.4   Spider's web presentation of the organizational pm competence   38
3.5   Maturity scale for the pm subprocesses   39
3.6   Sample question of the pm competence questionnaire   39
3.7   pm benchmarking results regarding the design of project
       organizations   40
3.8   Relationships between individual, team and organizational
       learning   42
4.1   Kolb's experiential learning cycle   47
4.2   Project management competence development and the Kolb
       learning cycle   48
4.3   Organizational project management maturity model OPM^3 50
4.4   Findings on the experiential development of individuals in the
       project-based firm   55
4.5   Attenuation of learning between projects   58
4.6   Findings on experiential learning in the project-based organization 60

5.1	Balance card for project team selection	69
5.2	Focusing on team basics	70
5.3	Goal matrix	71
5.4	SMART(IES) goals	71
5.5	Audit of team effectiveness	75
5.6	Project information board	80
7.1	Stakeholder satisfaction	101
7.2	Stakeholder identification grid	102
7.3	The stakeholder management process	104
7.4	Stakeholder resources	104
7.5	Stakeholders as change agents	105
7.6	An example of a stakeholder register	107
7.7	Stakeholder commitment matrix	109
7.8	Plotting stakeholder knowledge base	111
7.9	Tasks involved in gaining commitment	112
7.10	What affects the stakeholders' position?	115
9.1	The iceberg model of inter-cultural business analysis	137
9.2	The cultural onion	139
9.3	Role fluency	143
9.4	International mergers, acquisitions and alliances: the failure factor	144
9.5	Audit process for cultural due diligence	145
9.6	The cultural triangle test	146
9.7	Global alliances: managing cultural integration	147
9.8	Stakeholder mapping for projects	148
9.9	The Hofstede and Trompenaars cultural dimensions	149
9.10	Country ranking for project management	149
9.11	Conflict handling on international projects	150
9.12	Managing multicultural projects	151
9.13	Mono-cultural belief cycle	152
9.14	Cross-cultural behaviour/belief cycle	153
9.15	Cultural training and development planning	155
9.16	Transcultural projects – training and development strategy formulation	156

Notes on contributors

EDITOR

Rodney Turner is Professor of Project Management in the Department of Marketing and Organization of the Faculty of Economics, Erasmus University, Rotterdam, and a director of EuroProjex, the European Network for Project Excellence. He is also a visiting professor at Henley Management College and adjunct professor at the University of Technology, Sydney. After leaving Oxford University, where he completed his doctorate and was a post-doctoral research fellow at Brasenose College, he spent several years with ICI working on engineering design, construction and maintenance projects in the petrochemical industry. He worked as a consultant in project management with Coopers and Lybrand before joining Henley Management College. He has been with Erasmus University since 1997. Professor Turner works as a Project Management Consultant. He lectures worldwide, and has published several books and papers on project management, including the best-selling *Handbook of Project-based Management*. Rodney Turner edits the *International Journal of Project Management*, is Vice-President and past Chairman of the Association for Project Management, and is immediate past Chairman of the International Project Management Association. rodneyturner@europrojex.com

AUTHORS

Lynn Crawford is Director of the Project Management Research Unit at the University of Technology, Sydney, and Adjunct Professor in Project Management, UNITEC, Auckland. She is also Managing Director of Human Systems Pty Ltd. Through Human Systems, Lynn works with leading corporations developing organizational project management competence, by sharing and developing

knowledge and best practices through a global system of project management knowledge networks. She is involved in project management education, practice and research, having directed major collaborative research projects funded by the Australian Research Council and industry, on project management competence and management of multiple interdependent 'soft' projects. Ongoing research is focused on assessment and development of individual and corporate project and programme management capability. With a strong commitment to development of project and programme management as a practice and a profession, Lynn has taken a leading role in initiatives that foster global cooperation in the development of project management standards. Lynn is a former chairman of the Australian Institute of Project Management and of its New South Wales chapter.
lynn@aipm.com

Roland Gareis is Professor and head of the Projektmanagement Group at the University of Economics and Business Administration,Vienna. He is immediate past president of Project Management Austria, Austria's national association in project management, and owner of Roland Gareis Consulting.
roland.gareis@wu-wien.ac.at

Alistair Godbold is Business Systems Programme Manager with the National Air Traffic Services Ltd. He is a chartered engineer, a member of the Association for Project Management and holds a B.Sc. (Hons) in computing science and an MBA in project management. He has been a project manager for fifteen years, managing the implementation of business systems and business process change and high technology safety-related air traffic control systems projects. His interests include ethics and engineering on which he has written and lectured.
apgodbold@iee.org

Bob Graham is an independent management consultant and educator in project management organizational creativity and the implementation of change. He is also a Senior Associate at Primavera Systems in Bala Cynwyd, Pennsylvania, and the Strategic Management Group in Philadelphia. At the Wharton School of the University of Pennsylvania, Dr Graham taught project management in the Wharton Executive Education Programme. His work there stressed the importance of people in project management. He was also a Research Associate with the Management and Behavioural Science Centre. Dr Graham holds a BS in systems analysis from Miami University, an MBA and PhD in business administration from the University of Cincinnati and an MS in cultural anthropology from the University of Pennsylvania.
bobg@smginc.com

Martina Huemann is Assistant Professor at the University of Economics and Business Administration, Vienna, Austria. There she teaches project management to graduate and postgraduate students. Her research focuses on competences in Project-oriented Organizations and the Project-oriented Society. Dr Huemann is trainer and consultant of Roland Gareis Consulting and assessor of the International Project Management Award of IPMA – the International Project Management Association. She takes part in research, event, marketing and organizational development projects and is certified project manager. She holds a doctorate in project management from the University of Economics and Business Administration, Vienna and also studied at the Economic University of Prague, Czech Republic and Lund University, Sweden.
martina.huemann@wu-wien.ac.at

Anne Keegan is a university lecturer in the Rotterdam School of Economics, Erasmus University, Rotterdam. She delivers courses in Human Resource Management (HRM), Organization Change, Organization Theory and Behavioural Science in undergraduate, postgraduate and executive level courses. In addition, she undertakes research into the Project Based Organization and is a partner in a major European-wide study into the Versatile Project Based Organization, now in its fifth year. Her other research interests include HRM in Knowledge Intensive Firms, New Forms of Organizing and Critical Management Theory. She regularly presents at conferences on HRM, Knowledge Intensive Firms, and Project Management, and has experience of teaching management courses at Trinity College, Dublin. Dr Keegan has published a number of articles in leading management journals including *Long Range Planning*, *Management Learning* and the *European Management Journal*. She studied management and business at Trinity College Dublin, and did her doctorate there on the topic of Management Practices in Knowledge Intensive Firms. Following three years post-doctoral research she now works as a university lecturer and researcher. Dr Keegan has also worked as a consultant in the areas of HRM and organizational change to firms in the computer, food, export and voluntary sectors in Ireland and the Netherlands.
keegan@few.eur.nl

Bill McElroy is an Executive Director with the Nichols Group, a leading UK management consultancy specializing in project management and change management. He is a certificated member of the Association for Project Management reflecting his hands-on experience in managing projects. He has also led training and consultancy assignments in a wide variety of sectors. Bill has

twice won the APM's Sir Monty Finneston Award for his work in developing the management of strategic change.
bill.mcelroy@nichols.uk.com

Chris Mills is a senior consultant with the Nichols Group and has provided expertise and advice on managing programmes and projects for clients in the utilities and transportation sectors in the UK and overseas. He holds an honours degree in civil engineering from Imperial College, London and an MBA from Cranfield University and is a member of the Association for Project Management.
chris.mills@nichols.uk.com

David Partington is a chartered engineer whose career spans more than 20 years as a practitioner, consultant and lecturer in project management. He has experience of managing many types of projects for a variety of organizations in the UK, South America and the Middle East. He has an MSc in project management and a PhD in organizational behaviour. David is currently a lecturer in project management at Cranfield School of Management, where his research interests include project team behaviour, the implementation of planned organizational change, and context-specific approaches to corporate programme management. He is co-author of the Proaction project and programme management simulations.
d.partington@cranfield.ac.uk

David Rees, who professionally trained with UK Post Office Telecoms as a management services and work study analyst, left industry to pursue a lecturing career at Guildford College of Technology, where his attention turned towards the human aspects of communication. From this interest, David launched an enterprise, Cultural Fluency, providing clients with language, culture and management training services. Currently his areas of activity focus on cultural consultancy and training for large transnational companies, and the strategic management of his enterprise. He is an associate faculty member of Henley Management College, a visiting lecturer at many overseas institutions and a fellow of the Institute of Personnel & Development and a member of the Institute of Management.
d.rees@cultural-fluency.com

Tony Reid is chairman of the Special Interest Group on Project Organization for the Association for Project Management. He is a consultant in the areas of project organization and teamworking, and runs his own consulting, coaching and partner facilitation company.
tony@manach.clara.co.uk

Preface

This book is about the soft skills of project management, the management of the people associated with projects. I define management as getting things done through people, and so this book gives some guidance on how to get projects done through people. Historically, project management books tended to be very technical, describing the mathematics of critical path analysis, and earned value analysis. Over the years this has changed, with books taking a softer view on project management, recognizing the need to manage people. Several of my books have emphasized the role of project management in managing change, and the importance of involving and persuading the project's participants. There have also been books addressing the leadership roles of project managers. But few have given an overview of all the people skills associated with managing projects.

This book is derived from the *Gower Handbook of Project Management*, 3rd edition, edited by me and Dr Stephen Simister. It contains the chapters from the last part, on managing people on projects. To those chapters I have added two more. One is a strategic overview of competence to compliment the very practical chapter written by Martina Huemann and Roland Gareis. There is also a new chapter on learning in project-based organizations, describing how organizations can retain and maintain experiential knowledge to develop project management competence and maturity at both the organizational and individual levels. The book describes Human Resource Management in the project-based organization, competence development and learning. It also describes many issues associated with the management of the people on the project team, and other stakeholders. We describe how to make effective teams, and the role of the manager as leader. We consider the stakeholders, and the management of the conflict that can arise. We also describe the impact of different cultures, and ethical standards of project managers.

Chapter 1:   Managing human resources in the project-based organization
In Chapter 1, Anne Keegan and I describe the management of human resources in the project-based organization and how it differs from the old functional, hierarchical, line management organization. The chapter derives from a research project we conducted into the management of project-based organizations, involving companies from Europe, Australasia and Asia. We describe the evolution of organizations from operational to project based. We then describe selection and career development in the project-based firm. We close by considering how the pressures faced by project-based organizations are reflected in the Human Resources Management (HRM) practices they adopt.

Chapter 2:   Assessing and developing the project management competence of individuals
In Chapter 2, Lynn Crawford addresses the project management competence of individuals. First she gives an overview of different methods of defining the competence of individuals, and in the process describes different models of competence, and the components of competence. Then she describes standards for the assessment and measuring of project management competence, and shows how project management standards developed around the world, particularly by national project management professional societies, can be used to assess competence, and create models for developing project management competence. She then explains how the competence of individuals can be assessed as part of their career development. She describes how some organizations realize the assessment and development of project management competence. The work of this chapter is based on research she has done involving companies from the US, Europe, Australia and Hong Kong. The ideas can be said to be truly global.

Chapter 3:   Project management competences in the project-oriented organization
Roland Gareis and Martina Huemann continue the theme of competence development in the project-oriented organization in Chapter 3, giving a practical view of what project personnel need to be competent in against a project management process model they have developed. First, they describe the competence development of individuals and teams, considering many individuals who need to be competent. They then consider what we mean by the competence of the organization as a whole, linking it to project management maturity, and describing a benchmarking model they have developed to assess the project management competence of organizations. They consider how the project management competence of the project-oriented organization can be further developed.

Chapter 4: Delivering improved project management maturity through experiential learning

Many project-based organizations fail to develop competence and maturity, by failing as organizations to retain and develop knowledge at both an individual and organizational level. Anne Keegan, Lynn Crawford and I describe practices adopted by organizations to develop organizational and individual competence. They relate this to the maturity model first introduced in Chapter 3, and show there are three key themes of capturing experience in procedures, benchmarking and reviewing performance to further enhance those procedures, and developing project management mentoring and support communities. We comment on the efficacy of the practices in achieving learning through variation, selection, retention and distribution, and identify in particular the loss of learning through attenuation.

Chapter 5: Managing teams: the reality of life

In Chapter 5, Tony Reid describes the management of project teams, and how to make high performing teams. He gives practical guidelines on the development of high performing teams, describing team selection and the team charter. He then describes several other issues for achieving growth of the team, covering such issues as communication, personal growth and leadership.

Chapter 6: Managing and leading

In Chapter 6, David Partington considers the leadership role of the project manager, whether there is a difference between managing and leading, and whether leadership is something which can be learnt. Certainly good leaders can make themselves better by improving on the behaviours that work, and to that end David sets out some of the theories of leadership. He describes trait and behavioural theories, (two one-size-fits-all theories) and contingency and visionary theories, (two situational approaches). He illustrates how these theories apply to project management.

Chapter 7: Managing stakeholders

Stakeholders are all the people who have an interest in the outcome of the project. Some are for you, some against. In Chapter 7, Bill McElroy and Chris Mills describe how to manage project stakeholders. They describe a stakeholder management process developed from their work as project management consultants. They conclude by giving hints and tips for stakeholder management.

Chapter 8: Managing conflict, persuasion and negotiation

Sometimes the stakeholders will be just plain difficult, or they may have truly different opinions of the project from other members of the team. That can lead to conflict. In Chapter 8, Bob Graham describes the management of conflict. He describes how to avoid conflict, and resolve it if it occurs. He also describes the power of information in avoiding conflict, and gives a strategy for a project information system as a tool to avoid conflict. The key is in asking the right questions, not overloading people with the wrong data.

Chapter 9: *Managing culture*

Parties to a project can come from a range of backgrounds, from different professions, or different countries. Their different backgrounds can lead to different cultural traditions. In Chapter 9, David Rees describes the impact of culture on business and how it can be managed. This is based on his work as a consultant in culture and language. He describes the impact of culture on businesses and their performance. He then describes how to manage culture and cultural integration. He describes how to achieve cultural fluency by training staff in cultural awareness.

Chapter 10:   *Managing ethics*

Finally, in Chapter 10, Alistair Godbold describes business ethics, particularly as they relate to projects. Evidence shows that, in the long run, it is better to behave ethically, as it leads to better performance of your business. Alistair describes different ethical approaches, how they differ around the world, and offers some practical tips.

I would like to thank Dr Stephen Simister and Alison Pyper for their help with the original *Gower Handbook of Project Management*, 3rd edition, and Judy Morton for her help with this book.

Anyone interested in discussing any aspect of the material contained in this book is welcome to contact me by e-mail at the addresses given below, or visit our web page, http://www.europrojex.com

Rodney Turner
East Horsley
July 2003

rodneyturner@europrojex.com

Managing human resources in the project-based organization

1

Anne Keegan and Rodney Turner

We live in a world in which projects and multidisciplinary working are key vehicles for delivering corporate strategy (see Kanter 1983; Handy 2001). The increasing use of projects over the last forty years reflects rapid change in the nature of markets and technologies. Projects are spreading from the traditional strongholds of construction, aerospace and shipbuilding to all kinds of industries including the software industry, insurance, banking and education. It would seem that all industries can benefit from project-based working (Hastings 1993). The widespread use of projects as a way of organizing work has managerial implications for organizations in areas such as governance, operational control and the management of knowledge and learning. It also impacts directly on the human resource practices of organizations. Every time a new project is developed, the human configuration of the organization must change, demanding adaptability and flexibility from employees and managers.

Human resource management (hereafter called HRM) has a long and distinguished history stretching back more than eighty years to the pioneering work of the earliest practitioners (see Niven 1967; Megginson 1985; Paauwe 1991). HRM aspects of project-based working are among the key issues of strategic importance for project-based firms. In recent years, progress has been made in developing new concepts in human resource management applicable to different branches of industry and in different types of organizations (see Bacon *et al.* (1996) on small firms; Garrahan and Stewart (1992) on the international automotive industry). This represents a promising advance on the general prescriptive model of HRM evident in the early part of the 1980s which was largely dominated by ideas developed in the post-Second World War era. In this chapter we describe HRM practices and processes we have observed used for managing people in project-based organizations in strategically important sectors of industry.

FROM OPERATIONS TO PROJECTS

From the mid-nineteenth century to the immediate post-Second World War period the industrial scene was characterized largely by manufacturing firms organized along bureaucratic lines and managed through functional hierarchies carrying out operations which were stable and routine by design. In the decades after the Second World War the introduction of new technologies and materials led to a huge increase in innovation in industry. The scope of activities undertaken by firms widened considerably as firms sought to respond to changing consumer preferences. Innovation became a normal part of business activity, a prerequisite to survival instead of a fancy addition. Projects were frequently established to carry on this novel work. In the beginning these projects were isolated from operations and designed to produce something outside the normal stream of work (Burns and Stalker 1961).

Projects were a new undertaking for most firms and differed from operations as a method of organizing and harnessing human, technological and financial resources. Unlike operations, projects are transient. Unlike operations, projects are always novel and therefore, to varying degrees, unpredictable in their outcomes (Turner 1999). Operations set the status quo and rely on its being maintained for their survival while projects upset the status quo because they are unique, novel and transient. And unlike many operations that are capital intensive and rely on standardized skills, projects are heavily dependent on specific human inputs in the form of project team members who bring skills together in unpredictable ways. A cursory reading of recent management literature reveals that projects are no longer the isolated entities they once were. They are no longer the skunk works placed discreetly in the parking lot or the odd group of researchers working alone in an office far from normal workers and normal activities (Burns and Stalker 1961). Projects now pervade most organizations and have become accepted as a regular feature of doing business. In many cases, projects are the core activity of organizations and the centre of value added activity.

In observing HRM practices in the project-based firm, we have identified three core issues in successfully managing people in such organizations:

- selection in the project-based firm
- career development for a changing environment
- continuity and change in people management.

SELECTION IN THE PROJECT-BASED FIRM

The selection of people is an important issue for project-based firms. Variations in selection practices are evident according to whether the skills and knowledge of potential employees are core to the firm and not easily substituted or peripheral and easily found on the labour market. In many areas of project-based work, particularly traditional areas such as engineering and construction, employees are substitutable due to standard skills acquired through relatively short training periods. For example, several categories of construction worker as well as administrative, security and catering personnel can be considered here. Project-based firms often utilize these workers on a contract-by-contract basis or outsource this work to specialist service providers. In these industries, project management is the key core competence, and project managers have the longest tenure with organizations. In other areas, particularly high technology industries, employees are far less substitutable and constitute the core competence of project-based firms. Programmers in proprietary technologies, project managers and client liaison personnel are just three of the categories of organization members less easily substitutable in the short or even medium term and they represent the centre of value added for some of our case companies. Where employees are potentially core members of the firm, more time is taken to ensure that they are going to 'fit in' with the turbulent nature of project-based work. Selection of core staff – including technical experts and particularly project managers, leaders and supervisors – is conducted in a highly organic manner, meaning that emphasis is placed on informal methods of assessing people for employment.

The main practices used for selecting people to work for a project-based organization differ quite markedly from the functional, hierarchical organization and include:

- the use of headhunting both directly and through agencies
- the use of personal contacts and 'the grapevine' in finding prospective employees
- the hiring of personnel on project trials and work experiences
- liaison with personnel at universities and technical schools, often over many years.

THE GOAL OF SELECTION: THE RIGHT PEOPLE AT THE RIGHT TIME?

In project-based firms, we observed selection practices which Bacon *et al.* (1996) refer to as 'informally formal' practices. That is, companies have informal practices for managing selection, as shown in the list above. For most of the firms we have observed, finding the right people at the right time is not the most important goal when it comes to selecting personnel. People we have spoken to are on the whole cautious about the precision that can be attained in a transient client-led environment with respect to what it means to find 'the right people' and how sustainable such a definition might be. They indicate a more open attitude towards finding suitable candidates for their organizations and lay emphasis on the importance of supporting those people to grow with the organization and change as it changes. They tend to avoid go/no-go decisions in selection and emphasize selection by project, trial and work experience. Specific skills and knowledge sets are not as important as the adaptability of people to the changing environment within project-based firms and the willingness of organizational members to adapt as projects change and clients demand new approaches. Most of the firms we have observed avoid the use of selection tests in hiring decisions. They argue that decisions based on observing people at work, over time and in interaction with colleagues and clients is far more valuable than a go/no-go decision strategy based on one-off selection and assessment exercises.

PROJECT-BASED FIRMS AS FLEXIBLE FIRMS

In addition to hiring people 'gradually' through projects and trials, most of the firms we have observed use contracting as a way to cope with qualitative and quantitative uncertainties in their business. This is a type of selection for the short term. In a leading engineering and construction contractor in the oil, gas and petrochemical industry, estimates of temporary employees range from 25 per cent to 40 per cent depending on the workload. Respondents at a supplier of bespoke systems to the telecommunications industry estimate that at least one-third of personnel, including project personnel, are employed on temporary contracts to work on projects. Similar estimates were given for the other organizations we have visited. This mirrors the ideas of freelances and core peripheral workers popularized by Handy (1988) and others. In both these models, the use of contract labour is a central feature. An important area of future research is to ascertain more precisely the amount of contract labour used by project-based firms and the delineation of strategies surrounding contract labour. Numerical flexibility can also be attained by the increased use of part-time labour. As a twist on this theme, we have observed evidence of 'more than full-time' labour usage as distinct from 'part-time' labour usage as a strategy to cope with uneven workloads of projects. In one company we visited, project managers report work weeks of 60–80 hours. The potential for stress and burnout, particularly as projects often end up overlapping with no rest period in between, was reported by our respondents as an obvious tension within the workplace.

One implication of the use of high levels of contract labour in project-based firms is the importance of melding disparate groups of temporary and permanent employees into effective project teams. The successful achievement of this depends largely on how successful employees and managers are at coping with the disintegrative tendencies of project work and whether they display an emotional adaptability to new faces, new leaders, new colleagues and new conditions. Many firms use this as a strong indication of whether a new member will contribute to their organization or whether the relationship should be terminated early. In many companies, there is a pattern of newcomers leaving early in their probationary periods, whereas those with whom the company forges a stronger connection tend to stay for a long time. Although flexibility can be attained by surrounding a core of workers with a more flexible and dispensable periphery, the benefits may be illusory given the disenchantment of those in the periphery and attendant costs of training, selection and specialization required to maintain such an arrangement. However, project workers, especially those in the construction and oil, gas and petrochemical industries, have always worked in a transient environment. Project-based firms are transient firms because projects have a finite life span.

The potential difficulties of project-based ways of working are more relevant for those sectors experiencing a greater demand for innovation and higher levels of complexity. Resolving the tension of project-based work in terms of transience of employment is already a focal point for firms we have interviewed in the government and financial services sectors. In particular, the question of how to combine the machine bureaucracy with project-based ways of working remains a taxing issue. For those firms where this is relevant, there is an emphasis on instituting culture change, training and socialization programmes to make the transition to a transient environment of project work easier for all.

CAREER DEVELOPMENT FOR A CHANGING ENVIRONMENT

One of the clearest changes observable in project-based firms is the rapidly changing nature of career development and career profiles. Project-based firms in established industries such as engineering and construction are accustomed to shorter-term careers and the mobility of personnel. Organizations that have more recently adopted projects as an important form of operational control are faced with the reality that lifetime and long-term employment patterns are increasingly a thing of the past. Bastions of long-term employment such as universities and the civil service, as well as specific organizations like Phillips, Shell and Hewlett Packard, have all in recent years shifted towards shorter-term contracts and an emphasis on 'employability of staff' rather than employment guarantees.

THE SPIRAL STAIRCASE CAREER

The spiral staircase is the image that best describes the career patterns in project-based firms. Spiral staircases sweep upwards rather than ascend in a narrow ladder-like manner. The sweeping element of the spiral staircase represents the breadth of expertise and knowledge required in a multidisciplinary project environment that people must gather through a range of appointments as their career develops. This differs markedly from climbing the ladder up the functional silo, where people are developed in a narrow specialism. In six years with ICI, Rodney Turner had six jobs, covering the complete life cycle of process plant from feasibility to design, construction and maintenance. This is illustrative of the competence development required for the project-based firm, in contrast to the narrow specialization of the functional silo.

In conceptualizing careers in project-oriented firms, we are also inspired by the Dutch artist Escher and his representation of the monk's staircase that is constantly ascending and descending at the same time. Escher's staircase captures for us the challenge in the modern versatile firm that people must always learn and unlearn, both ascending the staircase of knowledge, as they master one set of skills and knowledge, and then descending to the lower level of a new learning challenge only to ascend once again. Career development in the project-based firm is also clearly dependent on the initiative of employees and their willingness to master new skills, often at short notice. In this environment, employees must take responsibility for managing their own careers and use their own knowledge and initiative to advance. Our work with project-based firms suggests that the reframing of career expectations is a vital aspect of the support firms can offer their employees in coping with the reality of customized problem-solving and project-based work.

REVISITING THE REWARDS ISSUE

Project-based firms are coping with a tension in their reward systems. This tension arises in the shift from traditional rewards, especially promotion 'upwards', to new forms of reward and recognition. It is becoming harder to reward people with promotion 'upwards' (and the prestige it affords) because hierarchies are flattening under cost pressures and under evidence that more organic forms of managing are appropriate in innovative, project-based firms. Project-based firms are placing emphasis on different types of rewards and encouraging employees to see development, and the prestige that normally went with promotions to a 'higher rank', in a new way.

One of our Dutch clients, a firm of engineering designers and constructors in the oil and gas industry, is a good example of this career reframing. It has developed a culture in which career development is couched in terms of projects of increasingly greater responsibility, complexity and challenge as opposed to taking a step up the clearly defined career ladder from junior to more senior roles. The company has broken the long-established link between number of subordinates and the value placed on a member of the organization. Instead of number of subordinates, the amount of risk a person manages and the strategic importance of the projects on which people are working are given emphasis. The company stresses the importance of people moving across projects, to different areas within functions. It rewards people who take on new roles in order to expand their skills even if it is not an upward move in a traditional sense.

In several organizations from the engineering, electronic and financial services industries, we have met people who moved from senior positions within departments to new roles which provide development of their skills and knowledge, and more responsibility for adding value for the organization and for clients, but which are not a move 'upwards' in the traditional sense of more subordinates or a 'higher' rank. A Dutch consultancy firm we worked with is also committed to the broad-based development of people and to the elimination of barriers to development including the shortening of hierarchies and the creation of a culture in which greater responsibility is taken as a hallmark of career development. In these firms, the spiral staircase career is widely evident.

DEVELOPING NEW MANAGERS FOR THE NEW ENVIRONMENT

Many companies point to the strongly held beliefs of managers as a barrier to changing career expectations. A Dutch telecommunications equipment supplier offers training to help managers deal with a new environment with flattened hierarchies in which they need to secure the cooperation and consent of project team members in order to operate effectively. There is a shift from viewing careers in terms of promotion and subordinates to viewing careers as continuous processes of learning and successful completion of projects. The company concentrates on training and development practices to meet the new needs that arise in a changing world. For that reason, team building and coaching are an integral part of training employees to manage new career demands. Project managers are learning that the goal is not to manage subordinates, but to lead experts and technical specialists in knowledge work.

DUAL OR MULTIPLE CAREER STRATEGIES

Von Glinow (1988) provides a description of technical career ladders in high-tech firms that is strongly mirrored in our experience. Dual career strategies have long been used by professional firms as a way to overcome the dysfunction of promoting technical experts to senior managerial and administrative roles (the Peter Principle, Peter and Hull 1969). Many firms have career paths for line and functional managers as well as technical experts and team managers. The telecommunications supplier mentioned above propounds a 'Competence Model' where the competence of staff is seen as a triangle. Each of the three sides of the triangle represents a specific type of competence: human competence, technical/professional competence and business competence.

Not all of the firms in our study have tackled the Peter Principle problem with equal success. In one electronics firm technical people cannot advance as far as traditional line managers and this is a challenge the firm recognizes must be addressed if it is to continue carrying out effective projects utilizing highly knowledge-intensive personnel. Respondents report losing valuable personnel as a consequence of their being forced into line and departmental managerial roles as part of their progression. This loss has promoted a reorganization, only recently commenced, with the solution of this problem one of its major goals.

We have also found a strong tendency towards the creation of more diverse career ladders, breaking away somewhat from dual ladders emphasizing technical versus line management careers. We have recorded the addition of career ladders in sales and marketing, and in the management of human resources. However, an unresolved issue which emerges from our research is the tendency for the uppermost layers of governance still to be drawn from one stream, generally that of line managers, as opposed to the other streams of career development. This may act as a barrier to the development and retention of experts in non-traditional management roles.

CONTINUITY AND CHANGE IN PEOPLE MANAGEMENT

Project-based firms face specific challenges in people management for three reasons. First, the customized nature of problem-solving places a premium on success in attracting and developing people. Project workers often have a high level of customer contact, as customers are often involved in the design and delivery of outputs, from buildings to software systems, from banking solutions to wireless communications. Second, project-based firms are temporary organizations. Because projects are always 'unique, novel and transient', the combination of knowledge, skills and abilities required to meet client needs is continuously changing. Third, project-based firms are insecure places. The gain or loss of projects can have an immediate and dramatic impact on the sustainability of employment, and the numbers of people needed. Project-based firms, because of customized problem-solving, transience in skill and knowledge requirements, and the fluctuating nature of workload, represent an interesting site for the study of people management.

These three features impact on career development and reflect broader trends in employment in society in general. The pattern of career development emerging from our study comes close to Handy's (2001) vision of working life for all of us in the near future. According to Handy, permanent careers are fast disappearing in all areas of working life. In their place, firms offer opportunities. These include opportunities to train, retrain, be outplaced or developed in new directions. Handy cites the case of Dutch oil giant Shell who announced its intention to cease offering employees stable careers. On March 29 1995 Shell announced its decision to become a federation of project-focused businesses and an ending of 'guaranteed' careers for those working as expatriates. This major restructuring of Shell's personnel policy mirrors the broader changes we are finding, indicating that new patterns of career development are rapidly becoming an integral part of the landscape. As such, those concerns being addressed possibly reflect broader developments to which more attention should be paid.

Our observations might also be interesting in terms of broader developments in HRM from a theoretical perspective. Secure employment is not a strong feature of project-based firms. This runs counter to two of the core ideas in HRM theory and practice.

The policy of hiring large numbers of employees on projects and contracts is at odds with the centrality of employment security which is a cornerstone of HRM theory and practice. This idea has a long history within the HRM tradition and emerged partly because of the difficulties faced by early mass manufacturers. The ideal of lifetime and secure employment was subsequently reinforced by Human Relations theorists in the 1930s who emphasized the importance of social aspects of work and the power of informal groups and their influence on firm performance. Maslow (1943) suggested that security was important in efforts to meet basic human needs and to act as a prerequisite to the development of worker commitment and dedication. The power of these ideas is still evident many decades later. Influential HRM theorists even argue that employment security is a universally 'best' HRM practice (Pfeffer 1998). They further maintain that it is necessary for the creation of high performance work systems. However, this may not be the whole picture. Notwithstanding the long tradition of adhering to the ideal of lifetime and secure employment, such an ideal may not be suitable in the context of the project-based firm. In any event, it is not practised.

The second HRM orthodoxy that may not be valid in the context of the project-based firm is that of the importance of employment testing and systematic

9

selection techniques. Employment testing is regarded as another HRM 'universal best practice'. It is taken to indicate that organizations value human resources and manage them effectively (Pfeffer 1998). Once again, we can trace this to the origins of HRM in the mass manufacturing paradigm, dominated as it was by ideas on scientific management and the attainment of effective 'person–job' fit. In every single firm we visited, selection takes place on the basis of projects, trials and work experiences. Headhunting is widespread and interviews are used to ascertain whether a potential candidate might be suitable for project-based work. All of this corresponds to recent calls by management theorists for managers to move away from the traditional emphasis in selection methods on the objective and the verifiable. Drucker, for example, has argued that managers must 'leap right over the search for objective criteria into the subjective' (Hams 1993). Sveiby (1997) also found evidence in his studies of knowledge-based, project-based and professional firms that intuitive assessment dominated all other methods of selecting candidates. Finally, referring again to a recent in-depth study of HRM practices in small firms in the UK, Bacon *et al.* (1996) found that managers prefer to manage in a way that protects the benefits of an informal and organic management system, and avoid the use of employment tests in every single case. Informality and intuition are an important part of selection techniques in project-based firms. Those firms in our study that have formalized their selection procedures tend to do so on a limited basis, formalizing, for example, the use of questioning on biographical or critical incidents, but still retaining intuitive assessment of candidates as the primary technique.

Our experience indicates that notwithstanding widespread theorizing on knowledge management, individual and organizational learning, this is still an area in which firms face great challenges. The practical difficulties of encouraging learning and promoting practices for developing organizational memory lag behind theoretical advances in this area. If our experience is representative of the picture in project-based firms in general, then the issue of learning must be a top priority for management as it is a strategic issue, but one for which there is much yet to be done.

CONCLUSIONS

The project-based firm has been with us for some time and it exhibits key differences when compared with functional hierarchies that dominated the industrial landscape for over a hundred and fifty years. Project-based firms are heavily dependent on individuals, many of whom are not easily substitutable because of their knowledge, skills, customer contacts and ability to operate effectively in a transient environment. Project-based firms have a variety of practices in the areas of selection, careers and learning that reflect the challenges and opportunities of project-based work, and face difficult issues in managing people. In particular, patterns of practice which exhibit an 'informal formality' may provide a key to resolving the tension between the need for systematic practices and consistency, on the one hand, and intuitive organic practices that nurture innovation and flexibility, on the other. In a world where continuous learning has become a prerequisite for survival, people management practices in these project-based firms might provide valuable insights for other firms who are increasingly project based. We hope the issues we have identified and the propositions we have developed in three main areas of HRM in project-based firms might serve as a basis for developing deeper research and a better understanding of these firms, and people management practices in them.

REFERENCES AND FURTHER READING

Bacon, N., Ackers, P., Storey, J. and Coates, D. (1996), 'It's a small world: managing human resources in small businesses', *The International Journal of Human Resource Management*, **7**(1), February.

Burns, T. and Stalker, G. (1961), *The Management of Innovation*, Tavistock, London.

Garrahan, P. and Stewart, P. (1992), *The Nissan Enigma*, Mansell, London.

Hams, G. T. (1993), 'The post-capitalist executive: an interview with P. F. Drucker', *Harvard Business Review*, May–June.

Handy, C. B. (1988), *The Future of Work, A Guide to Changing Society*, Blackwell, Oxford.

Handy, C. B. (2001), *The Elephant and the Flea*, Hutchinson, London.

Hastings, C. (1993), *New Organizational Forms*, Heinemann, London.

Kanter, R. M. (1983), *The Change Masters*, Allen & Unwin, New York.

Maslow, A. (1943), 'A theory of human motivation', *Psychological Review*, **50**.

Megginson, L. C. (1985), *Personnel Management: A Human Resources Approach*, Irwin, Chicago, IL.

Niven, M. (1967), *Personnel Management 1913–1963*, Institute of Personnel Management, London.

Paauwe, J. (1991), 'Limitations to freedom: is there a choice for human resource management?', *British Journal of Management*, **2**.

Peter, L. and Hull, R. (1969), *The Peter Principle*, William & Morrow, Toronto.

Pfeffer, J. (1998), *The Human Equation: Building Profits by Putting People First*, Harvard Business School Press, Boston, MA.

Sveiby, K. (1997), *The New Organizational Wealth*, Berret-Koehler, San Francisco, CA.

Turner, J. R. (1999), *The Handbook of Project-based Management*, 2nd edition McGraw-Hill, London.

Von Glinow, M. (1988), *The New Professionals: Managing Today's High-Tech Employees*, Ballinger, Cambridge, MA.

2

Assessing and developing the project management competence of individuals

Lynn Crawford

The competence of project management personnel is a subject of concern to businesses and individuals. Businesses realize that the competence of their employees is a vital element in corporate performance. Coupled with an increasing recognition of the importance of projects in achieving business goals, this means that organizations become concerned with the project management competence of their people. For individuals, job opportunities in project management and increasing demand by business for evidence of project management competence fuels concern for professional development in the interests of employability, career development and job satisfaction. Further, project management professional associations see the certification of the competence of practitioners as an important part of their role. Associations around the world have devoted considerable effort to the definition of a body of project management knowledge and the development of guides and standards for knowledge and practice as a basis for education, training and associated certification or qualification.

Whether for project management practitioners concerned with personal competence development, or for organizations concerned with the assessment and development of project management competence, it is important to have an understanding of:

- how competence and its components are defined
- what standards exist for the assessment and development of project management competence
- how assessment can be used in the development of project management competence
- what approaches are used by organizations for assessing and developing competence.

13

APPROACHES TO DEFINING COMPETENCE

DEFINITION OF COMPETENCE

Most of us have a general understanding of what is meant by competence. When someone is described as competent to do a particular job it is taken to mean that they know how to do it and have the ability to do it and to do it well. Generally, competence is accepted as encompassing knowledge, skills, attitudes and behaviours that contribute to effective performance of a task or job role. However, over the last few decades, considerable attention has been focused on competence and the term has acquired specific meanings for groups of people who understand and approach competence in different ways.

In considering project management competence it is useful to be able to break competence down into component parts that can be measured or assessed and, therefore, developed. It is also useful to understand what different people are thinking and the approaches they are taking when considering the assessment and development of competence.

THE TRADITIONAL APPROACH TO COMPETENCE

The traditional approach of employers when seeking to promote or select competent staff has been to look for the 'right' technical qualifications and a proven track record of doing the same job within their organization or a similar organization. Using this approach, appropriate qualifications and a resumé summarizing relevant work experience, generally supported by a face-to-face interview, are the basis for assessment of competence. A number of factors have lead to dissatisfaction with this traditional approach and have driven the search for a new way of selecting and developing human resources. First, the value of traditional academic aptitude and knowledge tests in predicting job performance has been questioned, as has the equity of such tests for minorities, women and disadvantaged groups. Second, this traditional approach often just doesn't work, particularly in project management, for a number of reasons, including:

- demand for such people may exceed supply
- the new project may be one that has not been done before by the organization
- the new environment may differ from that which supported past successes
- there may be factors in the individual's private life – health, family, other commitments – which impact on performance.

A further factor in project management is that many people with experience in project management do not have supporting academic qualifications in the field.

Project management is a relatively new discipline in which there are relatively few academic courses and associated qualifications and these are primarily at postgraduate level. Many project management practitioners have degrees in another field or discipline and have 'accidentally' found themselves involved in project management.

Two streams of thought, one in the United States and one in the United Kingdom, have given rise to different approaches to competence. The *competency model*, or attribute-based competency approach, has been most prevalent in the United States, while the *competency standards*, or demonstrable performance approach, has formed the basis for national qualifications frameworks in the United Kingdom, Australia, New Zealand and South Africa.

THE COMPETENCY MODEL OR ATTRIBUTE-BASED APPROACH

The work of McClelland and McBer in the United States, beginning in the 1970s and reported by Boyatzis in the early 1980s (Boyatzis 1982), established what is referred to as the competency model, or attribute-based approach. Followers of this approach define a competency as an 'underlying characteristic of an individual that is causally related to effective and/or superior performance in a job or situation' (Spencer and Spencer 1993). Five competency characteristics are defined by Spencer and Spencer. Two of these are known as surface competencies, namely knowledge (the information a person has in specific content areas) and skill (the ability to perform a particular physical or mental task), and are considered to be the most readily developed and assessed through training and experience. The other three are core personality characteristics, motives, traits and self-concept, and are considered difficult to assess and develop. Thus, according to the competency model, or attribute-based approach, competence comprises several competencies, as follows:

Competence = *Knowledge (qualifications)*

+ *Skills (ability to do a task)*

+ *Core personality characteristics (motives + traits + self-concept)*

Inherent in the competency model approach is the concept of threshold and high performance, or differentiating, competencies. Threshold competencies are units of behaviour that are essential to do a job, but which are not causally related to superior job performance (Boyatzis 1982). The competency model approach is mainly concerned with high performing or differentiating competencies, those 'characteristics that are causally related to effective and/or superior performance in a job' (Boyatzis 1982). For an approach to be used effectively in selection, promotion and development (see Chapter 1), employers need to know what personal characteristics, behaviours, knowledge and skills are causally related to superior job performance. Even when research has identified desirable attributes for a particular job role (Boyatzis 1982; Spencer and Spencer 1993), these attributes may be difficult to assess and develop. The competency model approach, used extensively as the basis for numerous corporate competency development programmes worldwide, sees competencies as clusters of knowledge, attitudes, skills, and in some cases personality traits, values and styles that affect an individual's ability to perform. Human resource professionals, in the United States and elsewhere, are most likely to think about competence from the competency model or attribute-based perspective.

THE COMPETENCY STANDARDS OR PERFORMANCE-BASED APPROACH

While the competency model or attribute-based approach assumes identifiable personal attributes will translate into competent performance in the workplace, the competency standards approach assumes that competence can be inferred from demonstrated performance at a predefined acceptable standard (Gonczi *et al.* 1993). The competency standards approach has not attracted the same degree of support in the United States as it has in the United Kingdom, Australia or South Africa. In the UK, it is the basis for NVQs (National Vocational Qualifications) (Weightman 1995) and in Australia, New Zealand and South Africa, it underpins government-endorsed national qualifications frameworks. Under the competency standards approach, competence is defined as 'the ability to perform the activities within an occupation or function to the standard expected in employment' (National Training Board 1991). Performance-based competency standards are essentially concerned with threshold performance, the minimum level of performance acceptable in the workplace, according to predefined criteria. Thus, according to the competency standard or performance-based approach:

> Competence is demonstrable performance in accordance with occupational /professional / organizational competency standards.

Reflecting the emphasis on performance in an occupational role, competency standards were intended to be developed by industry 'Lead Bodies' representing the employers and employees in the relevant industrial sector, occupation or profession. In Australia, these are called Industry Training Advisory Boards (ITABs), and in South Africa, Sector Education Training Authorities.

The competency standards approach has developed its own terminology, including:

- *Units and elements of competency:* describe what is done in the workplace, profession or role
- *Performance criteria:* describe the required standard of performance
- *Range indicators:* describe the context of performance.

Competency standards are written at a number of different levels corresponding to the demands of occupational roles and /or educational requirements. In these qualification frameworks, levels start at the equivalent of secondary school and move through to postgraduate qualifications, from entry level to chief executive officer. As an example, the Australian National Competency Standards for Project Management have been written at three levels, generally corresponding to the following job roles:

1. Project team member
2. Project manager
3. Project director or programme manager.

This approach has been particularly attractive from an equity viewpoint. It provides a basis for recognition of the competence of those who can demonstrate ability to perform but have not had the opportunity to gain qualifications required for entry to particular jobs, occupations or professions. This makes it particularly useful in areas such as project management where many jobholders do not have formal qualifications relating to that job.

The performance-based competency standards approach is supported by national governments in the United Kingdom, Australia, New Zealand and South Africa and includes well-documented processes for assessment against the standards. Assessment is done by registered Workplace Assessors, and individuals are required to gather evidence of competence against the standards from their workplace.

AN INTEGRATED MODEL OF PROJECT MANAGEMENT COMPETENCE

Attribute-based and performance-based approaches to project management competence place emphasis on different aspects of competence and therefore a combination of both approaches may be more effective (Heywood *et al.* 1992). It is useful, for purposes of assessment and development, to consider project management competence as comprising:

- the underpinning project management knowledge and skills (input competencies)
- the enabling behavioural characteristics (personal competencies)
- the demonstrated ability to perform or use project management practices, at a predefined standard in the workplace (output competencies).

Figure 2.1 suggests a framework which brings together the competency model (attribute-based) and competency standards (performance-based) approaches to competence, and provides a useful framework for identifying and measuring aspects of competence as a basis for assessment and development. According to this integrated approach:

Competence = *Knowledge (qualifications)*

+ *Skills (ability to do a task)*

+ *Core personality characteristics (motives + traits + self-concept)*

+ *Demonstrable performance in accordance with occupational /professional/organizational competency standards*

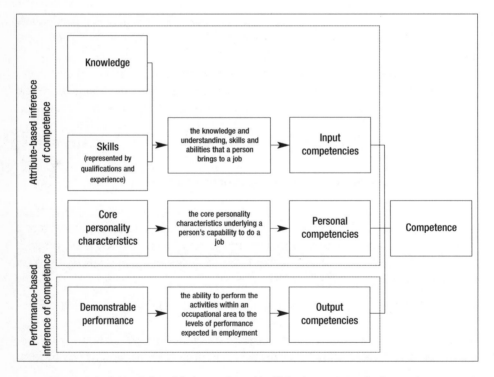

Figure 2.1   Integrated model of competence identifying key components of competences

STANDARDS FOR ASSESSMENT AND DEVELOPMENT OF PROJECT MANAGEMENT COMPETENCE

Assessment of competence requires standards or guides against which measurement can be made. There are only two aspects of competence identified in Figure 2.1 for which there are project management standards or guides that are recognized by project management professional associations or standards setting bodies. These are knowledge (input competencies) and demonstrable performance (use of project management practices, or output competencies). Standards are not available for behavioural competencies (personal competencies) associated with project management, although there is a brief listing of attitudes and behaviours expected of a project manager in both the Association of Project Management Body of Knowledge (APMBoK) (Dixon 2000) and the International Project Management Association's Competency Baseline (ICB: IPMA Competency Baseline) (Caupin *et al.* 1999). A number of organizations have developed corporate competency models for project management, identifying the behaviours that are considered desirable and associated with superior performance within a specific corporate context. An example of this is the United States National Aeronautics and Space Administration (NASA) Competency Development Framework, incorporated in NASA's Project Management Development Process (PMDP) <http://www.nasaappl.com/ilearning/pmdp/pmdp.htm>.

KNOWLEDGE AND SKILL-BASED COMPETENCE STANDARDS

Several project management professional associations have developed guides to the body of knowledge of project management, including:

- the UK Association of Project Management, APM, (Dixon 2000)
- the International Project Management Association, IPMA, (Caupin *et al.* 1999), whose international competence baseline (ICB) has been adapted into national competence baselines by its national associations
- the Project Management Institute, PMI, (Project Management Institute 2000), whose PMBOK® Guide has been approved as an American National Standard (ANSI/PMI 99-001-1999) and adopted as an Institute of Electrical and Electronics Engineers (IEEE) Standard (1490-1998)
- the Engineering Advancement Association of Japan, ENAA, (ENAA 2001).

These standards and guides focus primarily on management of individual projects, with ENAA's P2M standing out as the one exception. The P2M, developed with support of the Japanese government, specifically extends the focus beyond the management of single projects to management of programmes of projects in the context of corporate strategy implementation and enterprise innovation and management. Each of these guides is the basis for a project management certification programme:

- APM and IPMA have developed a four-level programme (Caupin *et al.* 1999). The entry level to this certification programme, Level D, is a knowledge test based on the ICB or National Competency Baseline, which in the case of the United Kingdom is the APM Body of Knowledge.
- PMI has developed a single level, Project Management Professional (PMP®) certification which includes a multiple-choice, knowledge exam plus project management experience.
- ENAA has developed a three-level certification programme which includes interviews, essay tests and project management experience. Qualifications are conferred by a Project Management Professionals Certification Centre (PMCC) which was founded in April 2002.

Project management standards, assessment processes and qualifications are presented in Figure 2.2.

PERFORMANCE-BASED COMPETENCY STANDARDS

Demonstrable performance or use of project management practices is represented by performance-based competency standards. These include:

- the Australian National Competency Standards for Project Management (BSX90)
- the United Kingdom's National Vocational Qualification (NVQ) framework (OSCEng 1997; CISC 1997; MCI 1997)
- those developed under the auspices of the South African Qualifications Authority (South African Qualifications Authority 2001).

Assessment against government-endorsed performance-based competency standards is undertaken by registered workplace assessors. Candidates are required to gather evidence of the use of practices in accordance with performance criteria specified in the standards. The workplace assessor works with candidates and advises and assists them to achieve recognition of competence. Candidates are assessed either as competent at a particular level, or 'not yet competent'. If assessed as competent, a candidate may be awarded a qualification recognized within a government-endorsed framework. The Australian Institute of Project Management has a professional registration process that is aligned with the Australian National Competency Standards for

Standard or guide (development body)	Level	Description	Form(s) of assessment
PMBOK® Guide (PMI)	PMP	Project Management Professional	Multiple choice exam Record of experience Record of education
	CAQ	Certificate of Added Qualification	Must hold current PMP certification Record of industry-specific experience Examination demonstrating industry-specific knowledge and skills
ICB: IPMA Competence Baseline (International Project Management Association, and member National Associations, for example, AFITEP, APM)	Level A	Programme or Projects Director	Self-assessment, project proposal Project report Interview
	Level B	Project Manager	Self-assessment, project proposal Project report Interview
	Level C	Project Management Professional	Evidence of experience, self-assessment Formal examination with direct questions and intellectual tasks Interview
	Level D	Project Management Practitioner	Formal examination, direct questions and open essays
P2M (ENAA, JPMF)	PMA	Programme Management Architect	Interview and essay tests Experience of at least three projects required
	PMR	Project Manager	Interview and essay tests
		Registered	Experience of at least one project required
	PMS	Project Management Specialist	Written examination

Figure 2.2 Knowledge-based project management standards, assessment processes and qualifications

Project Management and the Australian Qualifications Framework. Requirements for this process are available from the website of the Australian Institute of Project Management (http://www.aipm.com.au). The equivalent project management role, and professional and government recognized qualifications for Australia are shown in Figure 2.3.

PM role	Australian National Training Authority	Australian Institute of Project Management	
	Qualification	Award title	Post nominals
Project Team Member	Certificate IV	Qualified Project Professional	QPP
Project Manager	Diploma	Registered Project Manager	RegPM
Project Director/ Programme Manager	Advanced Diploma	Master Project Director	MPD

Figure 2.3   Project management professional and government-recognized qualifications in Australia

THE ROLE OF ASSESSMENT AND DEVELOPMENT OF PROJECT MANAGEMENT COMPETENCE

Lifelong learning is becoming increasingly important for project management practitioners operating at the leading edge of technology, who must be able to engage actively in critical thinking and reflection to transform existing knowledge, through creative responses and enhanced decision making, to meet unfamiliar situations. Professional standards and qualifications can provide baselines for knowledge and practice but it is the responsibility of each individual to reflect on their practice and actively seek opportunities to develop competence, raise benchmarks and improve performance. A model for assessment and development of competence is presented in Figure 2.4. This model is useful for individual practitioners as a basis for professional development. It is equally useful as a guide for corporate programmes for assessing and developing of project management competence. It clearly demonstrates the role of assessment in the development of project management competence.

As a first step, current competence needs to be assessed or measured. Guides and standards such as ENAA's P2M, the PMI's PMBOK® Guide, Australian National Competency Standards for Project Management, or IPMA's ICB can be used as a basis for this entry-level assessment and can be supplemented by using a range of personality, behavioural and other tests to form a picture of current levels of competence. Organizations such as NASA make a wide range of assessment tools available to their personnel to provide them with feedback on their own knowledge, performance, attitudes, behaviours and motivations. In corporate competency development programmes assessment of current levels of competence of project personnel can provide a baseline for evaluation of improvement.

Requirements of the job role form the basis for identifying the desired level of competence. This will ideally be documented in the job description, although comprehensive job descriptions for project management roles are rare and individuals may need to develop their own detailed job descriptions as a basis for competence development. In identifying job role requirements it is important to recognize that the project management guides and standards referred to earlier relate only to generic or widely accepted project management knowledge and practices and may only form part of the requirements of a job role. A full job description may need to include aspects of competence relating to the following:

- generic project management (represented by project management guides and standards)
- organization-specific project management (relating to corporate project management methodology, tools and techniques)
- organizational (relating to processes and systems specific to the organization, such as financial management systems, occupational health and safety, and so on)
- interpersonal skills (for example, negotiation, communication, leadership, teamwork)
- personal (attitudes, behaviours, motivation, values, and so on)
- technical (dependent upon type and scale of project, for example, IT, engineering, product development, and so on)
- business environment (for example, market awareness).

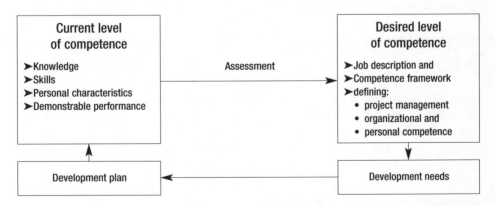

Figure 2.4 A model for assessment and development of workplace competence (developed in consultation with Carol Townley, Caliper, UK)

Developmental needs are represented by the gap between current and desired levels of competence. For individuals this can form the basis for a professional development plan. For corporate project management development programmes the difference between current and desired levels of competence of project personnel forms the basis for a gap analysis, the identification of corporate project management development needs and the planning and resourcing of corporate project management development programmes.

In the spirit of lifelong learning, reflective practice, career progression and changing workplace requirements, assessment and development of project management competence, according to this model (Figure 2.4) should be an ongoing developmental process. In corporate development programmes the process should be supported by:

- learning and development policies and resources, including opportunities for
  - self-managed learning
  - computer and web-based learning resources
  - work experience opportunities
  - mentoring and coaching
  - in-company and off-site training
  - professional and academic qualifications
- internal accreditation (matched to project types and external standards)
- performance appraisal and management systems
- career paths
- rewards and recognition.

CORPORATE APPROACHES TO ASSESSING AND DEVELOPING PROJECT MANAGEMENT COMPETENCE

Organizations can play an important role in motivating and supporting performance improvement. There are several aspects to this. One is the provision of a supportive environment – a project management culture, top management support, methodologies, systems, tools, recognition and rewards – that encourage effective project management performance. The other is the design and implementation of corporate project management competence development programmes. Design of these programmes should consider the need to ensure that all project personnel have the minimum levels of competence required for effective performance as well as providing opportunities for identification and development of superior performance.

Standards for knowledge and use of project management practices, such as the PMBOK® Guide and Australian National Competency Standards for Project Management, provide corporations and practitioners with guidelines as to the knowledge and practices required for effective workplace performance. Corporate performance can be enhanced if project management personnel are familiar with, and follow, such standards, thereby having a shared understanding of project management terminology and practices and the ability to deploy corporate project management methodology.

The author's research has demonstrated that assessment of levels of project management knowledge and use of practices against standards does not differentiate between threshold and superior performance. It does not provide a good indicator of those project management practitioners who are likely to be top performers. This is not surprising, as factors contributing to successful workplace performance are both complex and shifting. There are factors relating to individuals that cannot be effectively captured in standards or measured in examinations, resumés or in interviews, such as personality and behavioural characteristics, values, ethics and motivation. There are also factors relating to context, such as the nature of the project, the nature of the role, resource availability, competence of the project team, and extent of organizational support.

A practical approach for organizations is to use a standards-based approach to assessment and development of threshold competence of all project personnel and to employ other methods, for assessment and development of differentiating competencies or the identification and development of potentially superior performers. Brief case studies of these two approaches are provided below.

PERFORMANCE-BASED COMPETENCY ASSESSMENT AND DEVELOPMENT: THRESHOLD COMPETENCIES

The Project Management Research Unit at the University of Technology Sydney has developed a process for assessment and development of threshold competencies in project management. This is based on work with several organizations, and the results of research into project management competence using the PMBOK® Guide and the Australian National Competency Standards for Project Management. The process, illustrated in Figure 2.5, involves identifying current project management competency levels of staff through a web-based competency assessment process, that includes a knowledge test and self-assessment of use of project management practices followed by an interview with a registered workplace assessor. The interview with the assessor is intended to verify the initial self-assessment against the standards and provide feedback as an input to preparation of a personal professional development plan, which may

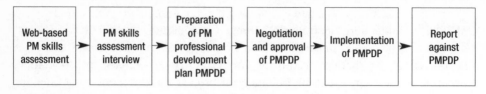

Figure 2.5   Process for project management development

include progression towards internally and externally recognized professional qualifications. These assessments provide a baseline for development and are related to roles and responsibilities, classification of projects and an internal accreditation system to identify development gaps. Individuals, in consultation with supervisors, and supported by detailed guidelines provided via the corporate intranet, develop plans to address the identified developmental gaps and work towards their own career goals. Once project management professional development plans are approved, it is the responsibility of each individual to implement their plan and to report on progress. Developmental resources available include reading and study guides, web-based support, mentoring and coaching, education and training, and work experience opportunities.

ATTRIBUTE-BASED COMPETENCY ASSESSMENT AND DEVELOPMENT: DIFFERENTIATING COMPETENCIES AND SUPERIOR PERFORMANCE

We saw in the case study above how an organization can identify the baseline competency levels of the majority of project personnel in terms of knowledge and use of project management practices, and then identify gaps to encourage staff to develop their competence. Having done this, the organization may wish to turn its attention to differentiating competencies and the recognition and development of superior performance. This may involve moving beyond reliance on generic standards for knowledge and project management practices to the development of guidelines specific to its own environment. These may include project management competency models identifying attitudes, behaviours and values that are considered to be associated with superior performance in that organization (such as the NASA Competency Development Framework).

The most widely used approach to attribute-based competency assessment and development and the identification and fostering of differentiating competencies, is the assessment or development centre (Woodruffe 1990). This is not a place but a process, usually designed to take from one to five days, during which participants are involved in a series of rigorous individual and group experiential exercises including presentations, interviews, problem-solving activities and simulations. Participants have an opportunity to complete and receive feedback from instruments that measure performance and effectiveness on different levels and from multiple perspectives, usually related to the defined corporate project management competency model. An important aspect of such centres is the involvement of highly regarded representatives of the senior and project management communities as assessors, who observe the participants during all activities, usually on a one-on-one basis, and provide informed and objective feedback and guidance for development. Effectiveness of the assessment and development centre is largely dependent on the willingness, dedication and commitment of the senior personnel, and their recognition that the process is a developmental opportunity for them as much as for the organization and its management personnel. Assessment and development centres are highly resource-intensive and expensive to design and operate. It therefore makes sense for organizations to offer opportunities for assessment and development of threshold competences, aligned to standards, for the majority of project personnel. It also makes sense for them to offer more in-depth, attribute-based approaches, such as assessment and development centres, to project personnel in the most senior or responsible positions or who are identified by their managers as having most potential for development.

CONCLUSIONS

Increasing recognition of the potential contribution of project management to enhanced business performance and the achievement of business goals focuses individuals' and organizations' attention on the assessment and development of project management competence.

Competence encompasses knowledge, skills, attitudes and behaviours that contribute to effective job performance and can be assessed and developed. Competence can be inferred from attributes (knowledge, skills and underlying and enabling attitudes and behaviours) or from evidence of ability to perform in the workplace in accordance with specified standards. Attribute-based inference of competence is generally associated with competency models and the assessment and development of differentiating competencies, or those characteristics that are considered to be causally related to superior performance. Performance-based inference of competence is primarily associated with performance-based competency standards and with threshold competence, or the minimum required for effective performance in a job role. The most effective assessment and development of project management competence will include both attribute- and performance-based approaches.

Project management standards for knowledge and use of practices have been developed by project management professional associations and government-supported industry training and qualification bodies. These provide guidance for assessment and development of threshold competencies, those aspects of competence (knowledge, skills, use of project management practices) that are essential to performing project management roles, but are not causally related to superior job performance. A wide range of personality, team role, attitude and behavioural assessment instruments and assessment centres are available to assist in the assessment and development of differentiating competencies, but are most effectively used in association with competency models developed by organizations to suit their specific environment, project types and job roles.

Development of project management competence will be primarily the responsibility of the individual, but will be most effective when complemented by organizational support and recognition. We deal further with how organizations can support the experiential learning of individuals in Chapter 4.

REFERENCES AND FURTHER READING

Boyatzis, R. E. (1982), *The Competent Manager: a model for effective performance*, Wiley, New York.

Caupin, G., Knopfel, H., Morris, P., Motzel, E. and Pannenbacker, O. (1999), *ICB: IPMA Competence Baseline*, International Project Management Association, Zurich.

CISC (1997), *Raising standards: Construction Project Management: NVQ/SVQ Level 5*, The Construction Industry Standing Conference, London.

Dixon, M. (2000), *APM Project Management Body of Knowledge*, 4th edition, Association for Project Management, High Wycombe.

ENAA (2001), P2M: *A Guidebook of Project & Program Management for Enterprise Innovation: Interim Translation of Selected Chapters*, Engineering Advancement Association of Japan, Tokyo.

Gonczi, A., Hager, P., and Athanasou, J. (1993), *The Development of Competency-Based Assessment Strategies for the Profession*, Australian Government Publishing Service, Canberra.

Heywood, L., Gonczi, A., and Hager, P. (1992), *A Guide to Development of Competency Standards for Professions*, Australian Government Publishing Service, Canberra.

MCI (1997), *Manage Projects: Management Standards – Key Role G*, Management Charter Initiative, London.

National Training Board (1991), *National Competency Standards Policy & Guidelines*, National Training Board, Canberra.

OSCEng (1997), *OSCEng Levels 4 and 5: NVQ/SVQ in (generic) project management*, Occupational Standards Council for Engineering, London.

Project Management Institute (2000), *A Guide to the Project Management Body of Knowledge (PMBOK® Guide)*, 2000 edition, Project Management Institute, Newtown Square, PA.

South African Qualifications Authority (2001), 'General Notice No. 1206 of 2001: Notice of publication of unit standards-based qualifications for public comment: National Certificate in Project Management – NQF Level 4', *Government Gazette*, Vol. 437, No. 22846, 21 November 2001.

Spencer, L. M. J. and Spencer, S. M. (1993) *Competence at Work: Models for Superior Performance*, 1st edition, Wiley, New York.

Weightman, J. (1995), *Competencies in Action*, 2nd edition, Institute of Personnel and Development, London.

Woodruffe, C. (1990), *Assessment Centres*, Institute of Personnel and Development, London.

Project management competences in the project-oriented organization

3

Roland Gareis and Martina Huemann

In the project-based organization, project management (pm) competences are not only required by individuals, but also by project teams and by organizations. These competences have to correlate. The pm competences of individuals performing project roles, such as project owner, project manager or project team member, have to be in accordance with the pm competences of the organization as a whole as documented in its procedures. The pm competences of individuals, project teams and organizations can be described, measured and further developed. As project management has to be considered as a core competence of the project-based organization (called in this chapter the project-oriented organization, POO), this competence has to be explicitly developed by the organization.

STRATEGY, STRUCTURE AND CULTURE OF THE PROJECT-ORIENTED ORGANIZATION

A POO is one which:

- defines management by projects as an organizational strategy
- adopts temporary organizations for the performance of complex processes
- manages a project portfolio of different project types
- has specific permanent organizations to provide integrative functions
- applies a 'new management paradigm'
- has an explicit project management culture
- perceives itself to be project-oriented.

The POO considers projects not only as tools to perform complex processes, but as strategic options for organizational design (Figure 3.1). Management by projects is the organizational strategy of companies dealing with an increasingly

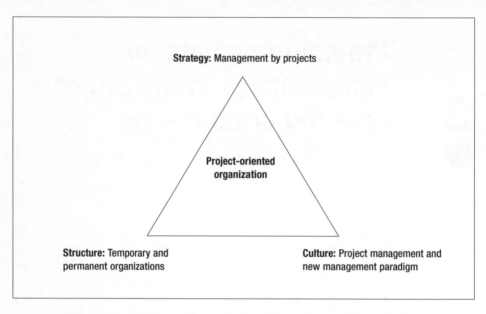

Figure 3.1   Strategy, structure and culture of the project-oriented organization

complex business environment. By applying management by projects the following organizational objectives are pursued:

- organizational differentiation and decentralization of management responsibility
- quality assurance by project team work and holistic project definitions
- goal orientation and personnel development
- organization of organizational learning by projects.

POOs perceive projects and programmes as temporary organizations for the performance of complex processes, such as contracts for external clients, as well as product development, marketing campaigns or re-engineering activities for internal clients. The more projects of different types a company holds in its project portfolio, the more differentiated it becomes and the higher becomes its management complexity. To support the successful delivery of individual projects, and to ensure the compliance of the objectives of the different projects with company strategy, the POO must adopt specific integrative structures such as a strategic centre, expert pools, a pm centre of competence and a project portfolio steering committee. Some of these permanent organizations might be virtual.

The POO is characterized by the existence of an explicit pm culture, such as a set of pm-related values, norms and procedures. Further, in order to manage a

POO successfully, the application of a new management paradigm is required. Traditional management approaches emphasize detailed planning methods, focusing on the assignment of clearly defined work packages to individuals, relying on contractual agreements with clients and suppliers and using the hierarchy as a central integration instrument. Compared with this traditional approach, the new management paradigm can be perceived as comprising the core concepts of lean management, total quality management, business process re-engineering and the learning organization, which are:

- organization as competitive advantage
- empowerment of employees
- process-orientation
- teamwork in flat organizations
- continuous organizational change
- customer-orientation
- networking with clients and suppliers.

PROJECT MANAGEMENT AS A BUSINESS PROCESS OF THE PROJECT-ORIENTED ORGANIZATION

By perceiving project management as a business process of the POO, the methods of process management can be applied to designing the pm process. By describing the pm process, by defining its objectives and by defining its deliverables, it is possible to measure the quality of the pm process. The pm process consists of the following subprocesses:

1. Project start
2. Project control
3. Project coordination
4. Management of project discontinuities
5. Project close-down.

Objects of consideration in the pm process are the project objectives, the scope of work, the project schedule and the project costs, as well as the project organization, the project culture and the project context. The achievable deliverables of each pm subprocess, such as the different project plans, the project culture, the defined strategies to manage project environment relationships, project progress reports, minutes of project meetings, and so on, can be compared with the resource requirements for the performance of the pm subprocess.

PROJECT MANAGEMENT COMPETENCES OF INDIVIDUALS AND PROJECT TEAMS

Project management competence can be defined as the ability to perform the pm process efficiently. The pm competence relates to specific pm tasks to be fulfilled, and it exists if there is pm knowledge as well as pm experience. In the POO, pm competences can be differentiated for individuals, for project teams and for the organization.

The pm competences required by individuals differ according to the different project roles they fulfil. The following project roles can be performed by individuals:

1. Project owner
2. Project manager
3. Project management assistant
4. Project team member
5. Project contributor.

The specific pm tasks to be performed, such as by the project manager, can be described in a role description. Figure 3.2 is a role description for a project manager.

The pm competence of a project manager is the ability to fulfil all responsibilities specified in the role description. Besides the pm knowledge and the appropriate pm experience depending on the project type, a project manager needs product, company and industry knowledge. In international projects cultural awareness and language knowledge are prerequisites too. The pm knowledge and experience required by the project manager depend on the pm approach applied by the POO. According to a process-oriented project management approach, the project manager requires knowledge and experience not just to apply pm methods but to design the pm process creatively. The ability to design the pm process relates to:

- the selection of the pm methods appropriate for a given project
- the selection of the appropriate communication structures
- the facilitation of the different workshops and meetings
- the selection of the participants for the different workshops and meetings
- the decision to involve a project coach
- the definition of the appropriate form for the pm documentations (project handbook, project progress reports, project close-down report)
- the definition of a project marketing strategy.

To perform successfully, a project team requires a specific team competence in

Objectives
- Representation of the project interests
- Assurance of the realization of project objectives
- Coordination of project team and of project contributors
- Representation of the project to the relevant environments

Organizational position
- Reports to the project owner
- Is a member of the project team

Responsibilities in the project assignment process
- Formulation of the project assignment with the project owner
- Definition of the core team members with the project owner

Responsibilities in the project start process
- Organization of the project start process (with the core team members)
- Know-how transfer from the pre-project phase into the project with the project team members
- Agreement on project objectives with the project team members
- Development of adequate project plans with the project team members
- Design of an adequate project organization with the project team members
- Development of a project culture, establishment of the project as a social system with project team members
- Performance of risk management and discontinuity management with the project team members
- Design of project context relations with project team members
- Implementation of project marketing with project team members

Responsibilities in the project coordination process
- Disposition of resources for the performance of work packages
- Controlling the results of work packages, ensuring the quality of work packages
- Approval of work package results
- Communication with members of the project organization
- Communication with representatives of relevant environments
- Project marketing

Responsibilities in the project control process
- Organization of the project control process (with the core team members)
- Determination of project status with project team members
- Agreement on or planning of corrective actions with project team members
- Further development of project organization and project culture with project team members
- Redefinition of project objectives with project team members
- Redesign of project context relations with project team members
- Project marketing with project team members
- Preparation of progress reports with project team members

Responsibilities in the management of a project discontinuity process
- Organization of discontinuity management process (crisis or change management) with project owner
- Contributions to the contents of the crisis or change management with project team members

Responsibilities in the project close-down process
- Organization of project close-down process with project core team
- Emotional close-down of the project and regarding the content with project team members
- Transfer of know-how into the line organization with project team members and representatives of line organization
- Final project marketing with project team members

Figure 3.2   Role description 'Project Manager'

addition to the pm competences of the single project team members. The pm competence of a project team is the ability to commonly create the 'Big Project Picture', to solve conflicts in the team and to agree on common project objectives. A project team needs the ability to cooperate in workshops and meetings. The common development and the application of project plans, such as a work breakdown structure, a schedule, a project environment analysis, and so on, have to be understood as tools to support communication in the project team.

PROJECT MANAGEMENT COMPETENCES OF ORGANIZATIONS

Not just individuals but also organizations have the capability to gather knowledge and experience and to store them in a 'collective mind' (Senge 1994; Weik and Roberts 1993). Willke (1998) describes organizational knowledge as hidden in the systems of organizational principles, which are anonymous and autonomous and define the way organizations work. It is hard to imagine that organizations possess a 'collective brain', but one could find the organization's knowledge and experience, for instance, in standing operational procedures, descriptions of work processes, role descriptions, recipes, routines and databases of product and project knowledge.

To describe and measure organizational competence, models of organizational maturity can be applied. The first model relating to the measurement of the quality of the software development process, the SEI Capability Maturity Model, was developed by the Software Engineering Institute (SEI) (Humphrey 1989; Paulk *et al.* 1991). During the late 1990s several specific maturity models to describe and measure the organizational pm competence were developed (Fincher and Levin 1997; Goldsmith 1997; Ibbs and Kwark 1997; Hartman 1998). Most of them are based on the PMI's *Guide to the Project Management Body of Knowledge* (PMI 2002). Traditional maturity models use four to five steps to describe and measure the competence to perform a specific in an organization. The scale usually used is initial, repeatable, defined, managed and optimized according to the SEI Capability Maturity Model (Paulk *et al.* 1991) (see Figure 3.3).

THE PROJECT MANAGEMENT COMPETENCE MODEL

The Projektmanagement Group of the University of Business Administration and Economics in Vienna developed a model of pm competence for self-assessing and for benchmarking the pm competence of organizations (Gareis and Huemann

Maturity level	Description
5 = optimized	● Continual improvement of process
	● Continual collection of data to identify
	● Analysis of defects for prevention
4 = managed	● Process is quantitatively measured
	● Minimum of metrics for quality and productivity exist
	● Collection of process experiences
3 = defined	● Process defined and institutionalized
	● Process groups defined
2 = repeatable	● Process depends on individuals
	● Minimum of process control/guidance exists
	● Highly risky in case of new challenges
1 = initial	● Ad hoc process, not formalized
	● No adequate guidance
	● No consistency in product delivery

Figure 3.3   Maturity levels of the SEI Capability Maturity Model

1998). The basis for pm competence is the project management process model described above, with its sub processes. For the description and measurement of the pm competence, we suggest not the steps of the traditional maturity models but a spider's web, with six axes (Figure 3.4):

1. Project start
2. Project control
3. Project coordination
4. Management of project discontinuities
5. Project close-down
6. Design of pm process.

The spider's web has the advantage that it is a multidimensional representation of the pm competence, allowing the maturities of different pm subprocesses to be visualized. The pm competence of a company or a business unit is presented by the shaded area, which results from connecting points of pm competence on the scale of the spider's web axes. For the pm subprocesses on the spider's web scale, four levels of competence are defined:

0. Not defined
1. Partly defined
2. Defined
3. Standardized.

These are described further in Figure 3.5. In traditional maturity models, the maturity level 'optimized' is usually considered too. Our pm competence model

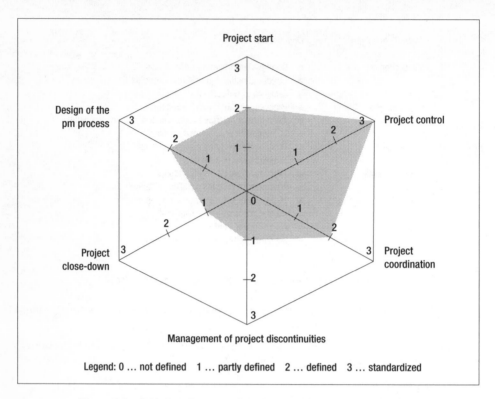

Figure 3.4   Spider's web presentation of the organizational pm competence

does not consider optimization, because it cannot be observed at the level of the single project and it does not apply to the pm subprocesses, but to the pm process as a whole. So the further development and optimization of project management is not part of the pm process but has to be considered as a separate business process.

Figure 3.4 represents the pm competence of a POO that has a lot of competence in project control, as it has a standardized control process, where it applies all required pm methods for all project types. The project coordination, the project start and the design of the pm process are scored 'defined'. Further improvement is primarily necessary regarding the project-close down and the management of discontinuities, where the pm competence is 'partly defined', that is only a few methods are applied for only a few project types.

The assessment of the pm competence of an organization is based on an Information Technology (IT)-supported questionnaire with about 80 questions. As an example, the questions relating to the project start process are grouped into questions regarding project objectives, project risk, project context relationships,

Scale	Description
3 = standardized	All required pm methods applied for all defined project types
2 = defined	Many pm methods applied for all defined project types
1 = partly defined	Few pm methods applied for many projects
0 = not defined	Few pm methods applied for a few projects

Figure 3.5   Maturity scale for the pm subprocesses

project organization and project culture (Figure 3.6). For the single questions the current pm practice is assessed according to the following answer possibilities:

1. Always
2. Sometimes
3. Seldom or never.

A weighting system is used to relate the answers to the questions to the competence points on the scales of the spider's web. As the single pm subprocesses have different impacts on the project performance, different weights are assigned to the pm subprocesses. The results for the project start process are the basis for all other subprocesses, therefore, it is perceived as the most important one.

B4.1: Which documents of project organization result from the project start process?

Question	1	2	3
Internal project assignment			
Project organization chart			
Project role descriptions			
Project responsibility matrix			
Project communication structures			
Project-specific organizational rules			
Project-related incentive systems			
Others (please state: ....)			

Figure 3.6   Sample question of the pm competence questionnaire

BENCHMARKING ORGANIZATIONAL PROJECT MANAGEMENT COMPETENCES

In a pm benchmarking research project with companies from different industries pm competence was applied (Gareis and Huemann 1998). Figure 3.7 shows the practice of nine companies regarding documentation in the project start process. Partners 1, 2 and 3 are from the engineering industry, partners 4, 5 and 6 are from the IT industry, while partners 7, 8 and 9 are from the service industry. The engineering and IT companies perform primarily external projects, while the companies of the service industry mainly perform internal projects.

Generally, we can observe differences in pm competences for the performance of internal and external projects and of different industries. A comparison for internal and external projects showed that in internal projects 'softer pm methods', such as the project scenario analysis and the project environment analysis, are applied more frequently than in external projects. In a comparison of different industries, engineering companies seem very methods-oriented, while IT companies emphasize the design of the project organization too. Some IT companies apply, for instance, integrated project organizations, involving client and subcontractor representatives in the project team and in the project steering committee. Project-

---

B 4.1: Which project organization documents result from the project start process?

Legend: ■ always ▨ sometimes ▦ seldom or never

	Partner 1	Partner 2	Partner 3	Partner 4	Partner 5	Partner 6	Partner 7	Partner 8	Partner 9		Best theory
Internal project assignment											
Project organization chart											
Project role descriptions											
Project responsibility matrix											
Project communication structures											
Project organization rules											
Project-related incentive systems											

Figure 3.7   pm benchmarking results regarding the design of project organizations

related incentive systems are used in engineering companies only. Furthermore, the following commonalities and differences could be observed:

- Internal project assignments are almost always a result of the project start process.
- Organizational charts are more frequently prepared by companies performing external projects.
- Project organization charts, descriptions of project roles and responsibility matrices partly do not result from the start process.

The column 'Best theory' shows the pm competence thought to be required by the Projektmanagement Group.

FURTHER DEVELOPMENT OF ORGANIZATION PROJECT MANAGEMENT COMPETENCES

Core competences, as defined by Prahalad and Hamel (Prahalad and Hamel 1990; Hamel 1994), are an organization's fundamental capabilities; an integration of skills that are competitively unique. This means that these capabilities are difficult to imitate. The core competences enable the company to deliver a fundamental customer benefit and therefore contribute to the long-term survival of the company.

Project management can be perceived as a core competence of a POO, as it creates a competitive advantage. If a company has pm knowledge and experience, projects can be performed more efficiently than in companies without pm competence. Project management adds value to the customer. To ensure this competitiveness permanent further development of the pm competence is necessary. Project management competences have to be described, assessed and further developed for organizations, teams and individuals. The pm competence model described above can be applied to assess the status of the organizational pm competence of a POO and to identify potential for the further development of this competence in an organizational learning process. Similarly, individual and team learning have to be organized. Instruments for the further development of the pm competences have to be differentiated for individuals, teams and the organization as a whole (Figure 3.8). Instruments to develop the pm competence of individuals include self-assessments and training (classroom, on the job). Instruments to develop the pm competences of teams include workshops, reflections and supervisions. Instruments to develop the pm competences of the project-oriented company at an organizational level include pm benchmarking and organizational development projects.

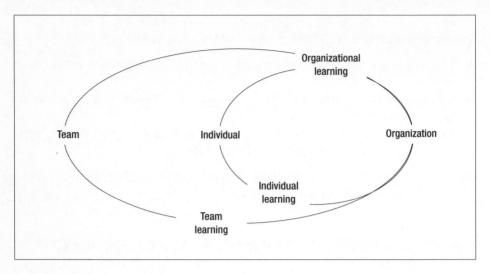

Figure 3.8   Relationships between individual, team and organizational learning

SPECIFIC MANAGEMENT COMPETENCES IN THE PROJECT-ORIENTED ORGANIZATION

Even if project management is established as a core competence of a POO, additional competences to manage further specific processes are required, such as:

● programme management
● project assignment and project evaluation
● project and programme auditing and coaching
● project portfolio management.

These competences must be described, assessed and further developed.

REFERENCES AND FURTHER READING

Fincher, A. and Levin, G. (1997), 'Project management maturity model', *Proceedings of the Project Management Institute 28th Annual Seminar/Symposium, Chicago*, Project Management Institute, Sylva, NC.

Gareis, R. and Huemann, M. (1998), 'A process-oriented pm-approach', *Proceedings of IRNOP III, the International Research Network on Organizing by Projects*, University of Calgary, Alberta.

Goldsmith, L. (1997), 'Approaches towards effective project management, project management maturity model', *Proceedings of the Project Management Institute*

28th Annual Seminar/Symposium, Chicago, Project Management Institute, Sylva, NC.

Hamel, G. (1994), 'The concept of core competence', in G. Hamel and A. Heene (eds), *Competence-based Competition*, Wiley, New York.

Hartman, F. (1998), 'Project management competence', *Proceedings of IRNOP III, the International Research Network on Organizing by Projects*, University of Calgary, Alberta.

Humphrey, W. (1989), *Managing the Software Process*, Addison-Wesley, New York.

Ibbs, W. and Kwak, Y. H. (1997), *The Benefits of Project Management: Financial and Organizational Rewards*, Project Management Institute, Sylva, NC.

Paulk, M. C., Curtis, B. and Chrissis, M. B. (1991), *Capability Maturity Models for Software*, Carnegie Mellon University, Pittsburg, PA.

PMI (2002), *A Guide to the Project Management Body of Knowledge*, Project Management Institute, Newtown Square, PA.

Prahalad, C. K. and Hamel, G. (1990), 'The core competence of the corporation', *Harvard Business Review*, May/June.

Senge, P. (1994), *The Fifth Discipline Field Book: Strategies and Tools for Building a Learning Organization*, Doubleday, New York.

Weik, A. and Roberts, K. (1993), 'Collective mind in organizations: heedful interrelating on flight decks', *Administrative Quarterly*, **38**.

Willke, H. (1998), *Systemisches Wissensmanagement (Systemic knowledge management)*, Lucius & Lucius, Stuttgart.

4 Delivering improved project management maturity through experiential learning

Rodney Turner, Anne Keegan and Lynn Crawford

In the last two chapters we looked at the competence of project personnel and of teams and organizations respectively. Further, in Chapter 3, the concept of organizational project management maturity was introduced. In this chapter we describe how project-based organizations can use experiential learning to increase the competence of project personnel, and the project management competence of the organization itself, thus increasing its project management maturity. Research shows that fewer than 15 per cent of project personnel have formal qualifications in project management (Crawford and Gaynor 1999). Thus, 85 per cent obtained their knowledge of managing projects through on-the-job experience. This raises the questions of whether this experience is effective in increasing the project management competence of both individuals and organizations, and whether it leads to increasing project management maturity. There is evidence that many project-based organizations fail to obtain experiential learning at both the organizational and individual levels (Pinto 1999). Pinto reports that many organizations repeatedly make the same mistakes on projects, because they have failed to:

- capture learning from successes and failures on past projects
- expose apprentice project professionals to learning gained in the organization
- encourage project teams and professionals to reflect on their own experiential learning.

On the other hand, Gibson and Pfautz (1999) describe success in improving the management of Information Technology (IT) projects within the Research and Development (R&D) department of a pharmaceutical company through the:

- formalization of the project management process
- adoption of post-completion reviews
- implementation of project management support and mentoring networks.

In the classically managed organization, individual and organizational learning is the realm of the functional hierarchy. Functions own and maintain the firm's knowledge, and provide people with careers as they climb the ladder up the functional silo. Individuals are exposed to the practices of the function, and learn the firm's business processes through experience. Project-based organizations, in reducing the significance of the functional hierarchy, lose its ability to act as a repository of experiential knowledge, and to provide experiential learning to individuals.

In this chapter, we describe experiential learning practices adopted by successful project-based organizations to develop the competence of individuals and the organization, and consider whether they contribute to increasing the project management maturity of the organization. In the next section, we describe the role of experience in the development of the project management competence of individuals and organizations, and how the project management maturity of organizations is defined. We then describe learning practices adopted by project-based organizations to structure learning experiences for individuals, and practices adopted by project-based firms to capture experience from projects and feed it back into the management of future projects and the development of individuals.

EXPERIENTIAL LEARNING IN PROJECT MANAGEMENT COMPETENCE DEVELOPMENT

Experience is the raw material of learning and knowledge creation, and the extent to which it contributes to competence development is dependent upon structures and strategies used by individuals and organizations to learn by experience. Kolb's experiential learning cycle (Kolb 1984) has become well accepted as a way of explaining the role of experience in learning, see Figure 4.1. The model shows experience alone is not enough. Experience needs to be accompanied by structured reflection and observation, leading to abstract concepts and generalizations, enabling the learner to develop theories for performance improvement. The Kolb model highlights the importance of experiential learning in project-based organizations where the unique nature of projects means the ability to test concepts in new situations is essential to competence development (see Chapter 2). Learning from experience is complex and dependent upon the learner, the task and the context. Experiential learning and competence development on the job requires an active partnership between learner and organization (Boud and Walker 1997). This includes the preparedness and skills of the individual to learn from experience, the work experiences, guidance, support, and encouragement provided by the organization, and the organization's

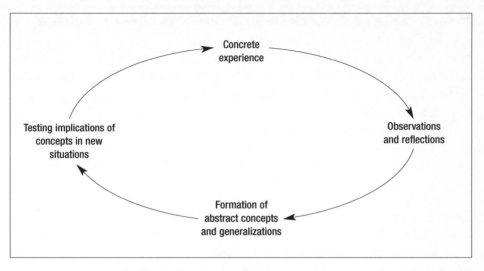

Figure 4.1   Kolb's experiential learning cycle

project management competence and approach to experiential learning in terms of its structures and systems.

COMPETENCE DEVELOPMENT OF PROJECT PERSONNEL

Experiential learning is a key contributor to the competence development of individuals and organizations. Most project personnel hold a qualification or first degree, but project management qualifications are rare, and an international cross-industry sample of project personnel found less than 15 per cent hold any form of project management qualification or certification (Crawford and Gaynor 1999). Thus experiential learning is the only source of competence development of the majority of project personnel, and so if project-based organizations do not make a sustained attempt to support the experiential learning of their personnel, they will achieve the outcomes reported by Pinto (1999).

Professional associations have attempted to codify the pathway of project management competence development through standards and certification programmes (see Chapter 2). Evidence of competence required by the certification programmes includes:

- academic and other qualifications (not necessarily in project management)
- exams (multi-choice, short questions, essays)
- self-assessment
- peer review through interviews
- exercises, tasks and simulations

- experience (project report, record of experience, portfolio of evidence of competence).

Figure 4.2 shows how this model of competence development of project personnel matches the Kolb learning cycle. It also shows where the organizations investigated by Pinto (1999) are failing to support the experiential learning of individuals (and the organization), and how the work of Gibson and Pfautz (1999) supported it. Evidence of experience is required by all certification programmes and is a key factor in determining the level at which certification is awarded. The most rigorous programmes are those associated with performance-based competency standards, including Australian and European programmes, and the United Kingdom National Vocational Qualifications (NVQs) (see Chapter 2). These require assessment of evidence of competence by a registered workplace assessor. The experience requirement of certification programmes highlights the important role of the organization in competence development and recognition. Unless project personnel work in project-competent organizations using accepted project management practices and providing developmental opportunities for staff, it will be difficult for them to provide evidence of experience necessary to achieve professional certification.

Kolb learning cycle	Certification requirements	Failures repoted by Pinto (1999)	Success reported by Gibson *et al* (1999)	Organizational development
Concrete experience	Project portfolio	To expose apprentice project	Post completion reviews	Project manager development
Observation and reflection	Self-assessment	To capture and reflect on experience	Post completion reviews	Performance review Benchmarking
			Project support and mentoring networks	Project community
Abstract concepts	Exams	To capture experience To expose project staff	Formalize project process	Information system Procedures
Testing of concepts	Interviews, exercises			
Other	Academics qualifications			Strategic alignment Management support

Figure 4.2   Project management competence development and the Kolb learning cycle

COMPETENCE DEVELOPMENT OF PROJECT-BASED ORGANIZATIONS

Not only are we concerned with the competence of individuals, but also of the organization (see Chapter 3). Although, as indicated above, there are widely accepted standards for the project management competence of individuals, there are no equivalent standards for the project management competence of organizations. This is currently being addressed through the development of Organizational Project Management Maturity Models (see Chapter 3). However, there is agreement that corporate project management competence requires the following (Kerzner 1998; Frame 1999):

● strategic alignment of projects
● top management support
● an effective project management information system
● clearly defined and well-formulated project management procedures
● project performance review and benchmarking
● a plan for project management selection and development
● an effective internal project management community.

Figure 4.2 also shows how these support the Kolb learning cycle. The organizational project management maturity models, try to define the project management competence for organizations by the level of maturity they have reached against the following three themes from the list above:

● processes and procedures
● performance review and benchmarking
● project management support and mentoring.

Figure 4.3 shows the five levels of maturity defined. The model is based on the SEI Capablity Maturity Model for software engineering (Paulk *et al.* 1991; Chapter 3).

Thus, experiential learning is the main vehicle for the project management competence development of individuals and organizations. The experiential learning of individuals should be structured within competent project-based organizations and relevant contexts. To aid this process, the organization needs to plan project management selection and development within a supportive project management community (see Chapter 1). To develop its own competence, the firm needs competent individuals and effective project management systems and procedures, based on project performance review and benchmarking, again within a supportive project management community. We describe experiential learning practices adopted by project-based organizations below.

No.	Level	Theme	Attainment
1.	Initial	Procedures	*Ad hoc* processes
		Review	
		Support	No guidance, no consistency
2.	Repeatable	Procedures	Individual processes for the most often used
		Review	
		Support	Minimum guidance
3.	Defined	Procedures	Institutionalized processes across the board
		Review	
		Support	Group support
4.	Managed	Procedures	Processes measured
		Review	Metrics collected, experiences collected
		Support	
5.	Optimized	Procedures	Continuous improvement
		Review	Data collected, defects analysed and patched
		Support	Continuous improvement

Figure 4.3   Organizational project management maturity model OPM[3]

EXPERIENTIAL LEARNING OF INDIVIDUALS

In describing individual development practices we concentrate mainly on organizations drawn from two contrasting industries:

- the engineering construction industry (ECI) with a long history of project-based management
- high technology industries, including computers and telecommunications, some of which are more recent entrants.

In the ECI there is greater emphasis on experiential learning, with formal education being given post-experience. In the high technology industry, individuals still gain most of their competence from experiential learning. However, there is a greater emphasis on early formal education, and particularly on certification. This difference reflects the lower maturity of the latter industry.

THE ENGINEERING CONSTRUCTION INDUSTRY

In firms with a long history of project-based management, considerable effort is devoted to the development of project managers. The ECI entails the mechanical construction of process plants in the oil, gas, petrochemical and power industries. Contracts range from $US 100 million to $US 2 billion, and have tight margins. Several features typify project managers in the ECI:

- It can take fifteen years to develop a project manager capable of managing a $US 100 million contract, and twenty-five years for a $US 1 billion contract. Potential project managers are identified in their mid-twenties and developed over these periods.
- Project managers are viewed as a key, value-adding resource, providing firms with their main competitive edge. Project management is viewed as a senior role, with project managers more highly valued than functional managers, and having the longest tenure.
- Most senior executives and directors of these firms are former project managers.

Development of project managers – the spiral staircase career

The role of project managers in the ECI is very eclectic, requiring a broad range of knowledge and experiences, including:

- management of the project process
- management of contractual relationships with clients, suppliers and sub-contractors
- management of the technology
- management of people in the project team
- management of the business
- management of different cultures for international projects.

It is not possible to develop people by restricting their experiences to one function. Thus, rather than seeing project managers climbing the ladder up the functional silo, they have broad, sweeping careers (the 'spiral staircase career', see Chapter 1), being exposed to a number of functions, perhaps moving back to functions in a more senior role. During their career, a future project manager may spend time as:

- a design engineer, in the early stages
- a lead engineer of a design team, starting on small projects, progressing to larger ones
- manager of the design function
- a project or contract engineer, progressing to larger projects
- an assistant project manager, then a project manager and, eventually, project director.

Managing the process of developing individuals

Although considerable effort is put into the development of project managers, like many things relating to careers in this industry, the process tends to be *ad hoc*. It is managed in two ways:

- through mentoring by the design department manager
- by an informal committee planning future requirements.

An individual's development is seen as a partnership between the individual and organization; the individual must take responsibility for seeking out development opportunities, but is supported by senior project managers, with opportunities for appropriate learning being made available. While individuals work as design or lead engineers, they have an annual review with their departmental manager, identifying future career aspirations, and development needs. That may include training or work experiences. Having identified work experiences required, opportunities are sought to satisfy them.

The organizations tend to maintain an informal committee of senior project managers and directors, who plan future requirements for project managers, and track the development of people within the organization. They seek out opportunities to match the development needs of specific individuals. A dilemma often faced is between keeping individuals working on their current project or moving them to appropriate career opportunities as they arise. Nobody is indispensable, and often people are moved to new projects that provide development opportunities needed. However, if a project is at a critical stage, they may be retained, and the opportunity lost. The fact that organizations are willing to move people shows commitment to the individual, and encourages staff retention. Several studies of employee retention found that employees cite development opportunities arising from project, function and divisional rotation as a key factor in their decisions about whether to stay with their employers. In response, companies like Booz Allen, Mobil, and Citibank build rotation opportunities into their career development plans (Bernstein 1998; Branch 1998).

The role of formal tuition

Courses for project managers are seen as an essential part of their development, but training tends to be post-experience. Project managers are first given experience on the job, and then sent on courses to enhance their understanding. New recruits are expected to work closely with the company's project procedures. Thus they are given formal guidance, on the job, about the correct ways of working within the context of the company's projects. Later they are given formal tuition in the knowledge behind those procedures. Early training is provided in-company, and relates to the organization's ways of working. Later training is more specific to the individual, and builds industry contacts.

The role of functions

Functional organizations tend to create a project structure project-by-project. The knowledge of the organization is retained within a functional structure, from which the projects draw resources. Thus the functional organization is significant both as a repository of knowledge for the organization and as a competence pool for projects.

HIGH TECHNOLOGY INDUSTRIES: KNOWLEDGE-BASED FIRMS

In high technology industries, the process of developing project managers tends to be more formal. Formal education and training, often linked to certification, plays a more significant role. These organizations view themselves as knowledge based, and often have a strong project focus – in some cases functions have been eliminated entirely. In these situations, experiential learning poses unique challenges. The projects tend to be smaller than for the ECI and are often part of a larger programme or portfolio of projects. Project managers therefore tend to be younger and less experienced, increasing the need for more rapid development through formal education.

These industries also suffer from a 'no home syndrome'. As projects are smaller and of shorter duration, people move quickly between them, working on more than one at a time. This also means that project managers do not tend to return to their functions between projects, increasing the sense of detachment from them. We spoke with one firm, the Viennese subsidiary of a global Information Systems (IS) supplier, that had eliminated functions entirely, adopting a purely project-based approach. There was nowhere in this firm to act as a repository for learning, and it was only able to take this approach because it received support from the European head-office, including its centres of excellence (see below).

Pairing and the creation of 'Nellies'

A common practice adopted to overcome the leaking away of knowledge and experience and to aid individual learning is 'pairing'. Where feasible, firms assign two people to a task where strictly one might do, especially a new task. This has two benefits. First, the two may develop a better, more innovative solution for the client, because two people together can work more creatively. Second, once the task is complete, there are two people who have knowledge of it, doubling the firm's experience. The practice of pairing reflects the immaturity of the industry. While 'sitting next to Nellie' (an experienced person) has been a training and learning practice for millennia (Plato mentions it in *The Republic*), there are very few 'Nellies' in high technology companies. So rapidly changing are the technologies and solutions these firms offer, there are few experienced people with whom newcomers can be paired to provide mentoring and coaching opportunities. 'Nellies' are created by pairing people who learn from each other through experimentation, rather than by transfer of learning from an experienced individual to an apprentice. Although there may be some redundancy, there is a greater chance that knowledge will be captured more effectively. This system ensures knowledge is developed and learning captured continuously over the project instead of simply at the end.

Certification

The absence of prior history is also evident in the strong emphasis high technology firms place on certification of project managers. The majority of people seeking certification from the Project Management Institute of North America are from the IS/IT industries (Crawford and Gaynor 1999), and many organizations from the industry use it as a key step in the development of project personnel.

Project support and mentoring networks

Another practice, reflecting the rate of change within the industry is the use of project support and mentoring networks, as reported by Gibson and Pfautz (1999). A common practice is a quarterly or monthly gathering of project managers, at which they hear about developments in the management of projects, also providing an opportunity to meet with other project personnel, and share experiences. These were most evident in the IS/IT industry, but are in fact used by firms from across our sample. The form they take varies, including:

- a quarterly conference held by a design and construction contractor from the telecommunications industry
- an informal, quarterly dinner-lecture held by the projects group of a Dutch bank
- membership of the European Construction Institute for design and construction contractors, the ECI providing regular meetings.

These project management communities fulfil an important role in the absence of functions, assuming some of the roles of a project management function, especially in distributing learning as we see later.

SUMMARY

Figure 4.4 summarizes experiential learning practices adopted for the development of individuals, showing how they relate to Kolb's learning cycle, and what certification programmes look for.

EXPERIENTIAL LEARNING IN PROJECT-BASED ORGANIZATIONS

In the project-based organization, individual learning is useless without practices to ensure the firm owns and retains knowledge. The firm can engage in formal learning – company libraries for instance – but must adopt experiential learning practices to learn how to manage the unique features of its projects. Not only do many organizations put significant effort into the development of project managers, but they also put effort into their development as organizations. Capturing, recording and disseminating experience are key to developing organizational competence and feeding it into the development of project professionals. In the project management maturity model (Figure 4.3), there are three themes for increasing project management maturity, which we have observed in practice:

Kolb learning cycle	Certification requirements	Selection in the ECI	Development in the ECI	Development in the IS/IT industry
Concrete experience	Project portfolio	Does the face fit?	Spiral staircase career Managed process	Pairing Certification
Observation and reflection	Self-assessment	Overt ambition favoured	Spiral staircase career Support networks	Pairing Certification
			Mentoring	Support networks
Abstract concepts	Exams		Post-experience training	Certification
Testing of concepts	Interviews, exercises	Staff used as contractors initially	Spiral staircase career	Certification
Other	Academic qualifications	Engineering qualifications favoured		

Figure 4.4 Findings on the experiential development of individuals in the project-based firm

1. the use of internal project management procedures and systems
2. project performance review, including:
   - end of project reviews
   - benchmarking
3. distribution of the learning through support networks, including:
   - project management self-support groups or conferences
   - the use of the intranet
   - centres of excellence
   - moving people around the organization.

INTERNAL PROJECT MANAGEMENT PROCEDURES

Internal project management procedures are a key way for organizations to capture knowledge and experience. They are the collective representation of the firm's experiences. Ericsson has a procedure called PROPS, first published in 1987, now in its third edition. The product development manager for PROPS is located at Ericsson's project management headquarters in Stockholm. The UK government has developed PRINCE 2 (CCTA 1996). PRINCE 2 certification is becoming mandatory to bid for many projects in the public and private sector. In this way the government is contributing not only to the increasing competence of public sector projects through capturing of best practice, but also to increasing project management competence of the society.

Most organizations treat the procedures as flexible guidelines, to be tailored to individual projects. Every project is different, and so requires a unique procedure (Payne and Turner 1999). Standard procedures represent captured experience and best practice, but need to be tailored project-by-project. Part of a project manager's tacit knowledge built up through experience (Polanyi 1967) enables them to know how procedures need to be tailored to the needs of individual projects. People with the lack of maturity that makes them want to follow procedures to the letter are not yet ready to be project managers. One firm from the ECI requires new project personnel to follow procedures strictly on their first project (when they will be in a support role, 'sitting next to Nellie'). On subsequent projects, they can reduce the amount they refer to the documentation as they internalize the firm's good practice. They may then adapt the procedures to the needs of the individual projects.

The emphasis on procedures, both as a learning medium and a measure of maturity, tends to emphasize process over outcome (Levitt and March 1995). ISO 10,006 (ISO 1997) says that both process and outcome should be emphasized on projects, and an emphasis on one is not mutually exclusive of the other. Project managers need to learn to focus on both, and Pinto (1999) describes what happens when there is a lack of focus on process. The emphasis on procedure can also lead to redundancy of experience and competency traps (Levitt and March 1995) where inferior procedures are reinforced and superior ones never discovered. However, the need to develop project-specific procedures for each project should ensure new processes are tried. The latter encourages variation, although many project-based organizations are very conservative. The ECI, in particular, being a safety critical industry with tight margins and dominant clients, prefers reliability over innovation.

END OF PROJECT REVIEWS

End of project reviews play a vital part in capturing experience. Many organizations' procedures, including Ericsson's PROPS process, require this. Figure 4.3 shows that, at higher levels of maturity, organizations continually benchmark their procedures and processes, gathering data about project performance and storing it as historical data to help plan future projects, thereby improving overall project performance. However, there is less than satisfactory use of end project reviews. Many firms find the practice difficult to enforce, and where it is enforced, it is a meaningless box-ticking exercise. A contractor from the Information and Communications Technology Industry reported that post-completion reviews were an essential part of their quality assurance procedures, but there was no check on the quality of the outputs. Further, where reviews are conducted, it can be difficult to transmit the learning to the organization, for three reasons:

1. A project may last for several years. Valuable learning experiences take place at the beginning of the project, but are not captured until the post-project review at the end, if at all.
2. When learning is successfully captured, it needs to be transmitted to the organization. Updating internal procedures may achieve that. However, it may be several years between issues of the procedures, delaying distribution of the learning. A more subtle problem is how to ensure people work to the current version. People become less reliant on the procedures as their experience grows, so they may not quickly assimilate the new issues. We discuss below practices adopted to distribute learning in other ways.
3. There is attenuation of the learning as it passes from one project to the next. New knowledge from the current project (variation) is captured in the end of project review (selection), recorded (retention), and then passed to new projects (distribution). Figure 4.5 shows attenuation in knowledge at each step (Cooke-Davies 2001). In the functional organization, learning is captured in the function, so attenuation is not a problem.

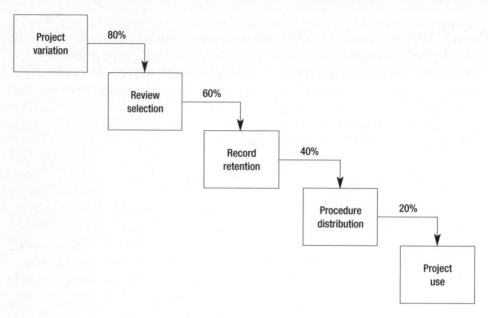

Figure 4.5   Attenuation of learning between projects

BENCHMARKING

Another method is benchmarking project performance. It is usually not effective to benchmark projects internally, but against projects undertaken by other firms in the industry. Gareis and Huemann (Chapter 3) describe benchmarking of high technology companies and projects. The European Construction Institute and the American Construction Industry Institute are benchmarking projects in the ECI in the two continents, and have about 4000 projects in their database.

DISTRIBUTING EXPERIENTIAL LEARNING

We saw above that there can be a delay between learning experiences being gained on projects and being captured in post-completion reviews. Further delay and attenuation occur between experiential learning being captured and recorded in the new project procedures and their dissemination and adoption. Successful project-based organizations adopt practices to ensure the learning experiences are gained by the organization at large before they are eventually reflected in the procedures. This is essential in the absence of functions. If we view a project as a temporary organization, then a project-based organization is a community of projects. The projects, as temporary organizations, will learn from each other by normative, coercive and mimetic processes (Levitt and March 1995). We see all of these being used in project-based organizations with project management communities, centres of excellence and transfer of people around the organization respectively. The use of the intranet may also be a coercive process.

Project management self-support groups or conferences

We discussed the role of self-support groups as part of individual learning. We see again their significance in fulfilling the role of the functions where functions are of reduced significance.

The use of the intranet

Many organizations are experimenting with the use of the intranet (Cooper *et al.* 2002). Ericsson has developed the concept of the virtual project office on a central server, supported by a powerful search engine. Project plans, progress reports, issues registers, and so on, are posted in the e-project office. Someone with a similar project or problem can search and interrogate existing or completed projects. It is up to the person with the problem to search. This is different from what Digital Equipment Corp. did in the early 1990s. There a person with a problem would e-mail everybody else in the organization, and it was up to the person with the solution to respond. This often did not work because the people with the solutions were too busy.

There is, however, an issue with the viscosity of knowledge and learning. We saw above the problem of deferral – learning taking years to spread to the organization. With the intranet it can spread too quickly; yesterday's hearsay can become today's perceived wisdom. Cooper *et al.* (2002) suggest that it is essential to have gatekeepers who review all information before it is posted on the intranet; this is fine, but expensive, and yet to be tested.

Centres of excellence and international programmes

Many of the firms we studied are global, with international mechanisms for retaining learning and disseminating it throughout the company. There are two main practices. First are international centres of excellence in specific project processes. Second are international programmes on issues of specific importance to companies at a given time. The centres offer advice to operating companies and record changes in standard practice. For example, within Ericsson, the Project Management Institute in Stockholm is responsible for maintaining their PROPS procedure and running the quarterly conference discussed above. Where local deviations are examined and determined to be successful, the centres of excellence will codify these, provide training, and retain the learning within the company.

Moving people around the organization

Another technique for spreading experience is to move people around the organization. By posting people in another town or country, experience is transferred as people make contacts with new colleagues. This is a slow but effective method.

The role of functions

Most of the organizations have not eliminated functions. The functions remain in a central competence pool, to act as a service and supplier of resources to projects. Functions appear to be essential to the learning and development of individuals and organizations. As we have seen, there are various specialist forms of functions used, such as self-support networks and centres of excellence.

SUMMARY

Figure 4.6 shows how our observations compare with the theory of development of project-based organizations as presented in Figure 4.2.

Kolb learning cycle	Theory from Table 1	Theory observed	Theory not observed	Other practices observed
Concrete experience	Project manager development	Yes		Pairing Overseas postings
Observation and reflection	Project community	Networks Conferences		Post completion review Benchmarking
Abstract concepts	Procedures Information system	Used intranet		Centres of excellence
Testing of concepts				
General	Strategic alignment Management support	Networks	Not mentioned	

Figure 4.6   Findings on experiential learning in the project-based organization

CONCLUSIONS

We have seen that the experiential learning practices adopted by project-based organizations match the three themes of increasing organizational project management maturity (see Figure 4.3):

- recording organizational learning through project management procedures
- capturing experiences through post-completion reviews, and improving knowledge through comparison, benchmarking and metrics
- distributing learning through project management support networks, communities and knowledge.

PROCEDURES

Procedures are the main way organizations retain and distribute knowledge. Procedures can also be tools for variation and selection, allowing new approaches to be incorporated, and deciding which should be retained. However, they can also be competency traps, preventing variation. The centralization of procedure maintenance is a strength, as it ensures consistency of learning. However, it is the responsibility of the project teams to develop the project-specific version of them, ensuring learning is distributed. Tsai (2001) reports that a business unit's ability to learn is dependent on its centrality and absorptive capacity. We see the project management function trying to increase the centrality of project learning, but in the process reduce absorptive capacity. The main problem is one of attenuation and deferral. Ericsson published the first and second edition of its PROPS procedure two years apart in the 1980s. The third edition was published six years later in the early 1990s, and Ericsson is working on the fourth edition now. Between the second and third and fourth editions there is a potential six-year delay before new learning is incorporated. A similar pattern is evident in the UK Government's PRINCE 2 process. However, there is a balance between changes being too rapid and too slow, (viscosity of information). The procedures are repositories of knowledge that has been tried and tested and proven to work, (the role of the functions in the classically managed organization). They primarily fulfil the roles of selection and retention, and not variation, and hence slow changes are appropriate. PRINCE 2 achieves this through occasional patches between editions.

REVIEWS

The role of reviews is selection of learning for retention. Projects are the vehicles for variation and, through reviews, project teams select those learning experiences for recording and distribution. There are two problems, however. The first is they are not centralized. They are the responsibility of the project teams, and often do not happen due to the pressure of the next project, even though they are nominally compulsory in many organizations. The other is attenuation and deferral of the learning. Only 20 per cent of learning reaches new projects (see Figure 4.5). It is in review that the greatest weakness occurs in experiential learning. There are organizations that would claim to be at level 3 or 4 in maturity, and their use of procedures and distribution of learning would justify that. However, they fail to achieve continuous improvement because of their failure to review. Kolb's learning cycle is broken at reflection.

SUPPORT COMMUNITIES

The role of project management communities is distribution of knowledge. They replace the functions in the traditional organization in that role. We have seen that, because it is appropriate that updates to the company's procedures should be infrequent to provide stability, the communities are the method of achieving more rapid distribution of current knowledge. Attenuation of project management learning (see Figure 4.5) would suggest the communities are not working as well as they might, but the fact that 20 per cent of learning is reaching future projects would suggest they have some effect. The use of communities both centralizes project management learning, and increases its absorptive capacity.

REFERENCES AND FURTHER READING

Bernstein, A. (1998), 'We want you to stay: really', *Business Week*, June 22.

Boud, D. and Walker, D. (1997), *Experience and Learning in the Workplace: Reflection at Work*, Deakin University, Geelong, Victoria.

Branch, S. (1998), 'You hired 'em, but can you keep 'em?', *Fortune*, November 9.

CCTA (1996), *PRINCE 2: Project Management for Business*, The Stationery Office, London.

Cooke-Davies, T. (2001), 'Project close-out management – more than just "good-bye" and move on', in D. Hilson and T. M. Williams, (eds), *A Project Management Odyssey, Proceedings of PMI Europe 2001*, PMI UK Chapter, London.

Cooper, K., Lyneis, J., and Bryant, B. (2002), 'Learning to learn, from past to future', *International Journal of Project Management*, **20**(3).

Crawford, L and Gaynor, F. (1999), 'Assessing and developing project management competence', *Learning, Knowledge, Wisdom, Proceedings of the 30th Annual PMI Seminars and Symposium, Philadelphia*, Project Management Institute, Sylva, NC.

Frame, J. D. (1999), *Project Management Competence: Building Skills for Individuals, Teams and Organizations*, Jossey-Bass Publishers, San Francisco.

Gibson, L. R. and Pfautz, S. (1999), 'Re-engineering IT project management in an R&D organization – a case study', in K. A. Arrto, K. Kähkönen and K. Koskinnen, (eds) *Managing Business by Projects, Proceedings of the NORDNET Symposium*, University of Technology, Helsinki.

ISO (1997), *ISO10,006: Quality Management – Guidelines to Quality in Project Management*, International Standards Organization, Geneva.

Kerzner, H. (1998), *In search of excellence in project management: successful practices in high performance organizations*, Van Nostrand Reinhold, New York.

Kolb, D. A. (1984), *Experiential Learning: Experience as the Source of Learning and Development*, Prentice-Hall, Englewood Cliffs, NJ.

Levitt, B., and March, J.G. (1995), 'Chester I Barnard and the intelligence of learning', in O. E. Williamson, *Organization Theory: from Chester Barnard to the present and beyond, expanded edition*, Oxford University Press, New York.

Paulk, M. C., Curtis, B., and Chrissis, M. B. (1991), *Capability Maturity Models for Software*, Carnegie Melon University, Pittsburg, PA.

Payne, J. H. and Turner, J. R. (1999), 'Company-wide project management: the planning and control of programmes of projects of different types', *International Journal of Project Management* **17**(1): 55–60.

Pinto, J. K. (1999), 'Managing information systems projects: regaining control of a runaway train', in K. A. Arrto, K. Kähkönen and K. Koskinnen, (eds) *Managing Business by Projects, Proceedings of the NORDNET Symposium*, University of Technology, Helsinki.

Polanyi, M. (1967), *The Tacit Dimension*, Doubleday Anchor, New York.

Tsai, W. (2001), 'Knowledge transfer in intraorganizational networks: effects of network position and absorptive capacity on business unit innovation and performance', *The Academy of Management Journal*, **44**(5): 996–1004.

5 Managing teams: the reality of life

Tony Reid

Everyone agrees that project teams are a good idea: true or false? Most teams start out full of energy, with good intentions and often offers of support. Unfortunately, fairly quickly things begin to look less certain. The consequence is that, instead of a surge of energy, there is a feeling of being alone, neglected, attacked even. The goals that were once clear now seem conditional on all sorts of other factors, while the sources of authority are joined by more shadowy influencers in the background who appear to be the ones who really call the shots. The next move is that team members are re-assigned back to their home base or to higher priority projects, often halfway through the assignment. Deadlines become immovable and unachievable, overtime and exhaustion set in. Management re-organizes the project team in exasperation, and demotivated people begin to fulfil every prophecy. At this moment you may be nodding your head as you recognize this as a familiar experience. The key question is why, and what can be done to avoid it happening?

It is with this scenario in mind that this chapter sets out to provide some basic, proven guidelines to help you create a capable project team. The guidelines do not require you to be a team development specialist: many organizations have halted their efforts in going in this direction because they were too costly, didn't provide quick enough results or were poorly understood by management. A warning for you: management has good intentions but poor follow-through due to pressures to produce quick results.

In reality many organizations are poor at project management and project leaders equally poor at team building. In the former instance, it is because there is insufficient discipline at pre-commencement, and in the latter it is because in creating a project the project leader does not see the team as a priority. Responding to the client, leaping into action, often with no apparent direction, is more likely to be the norm.

RESULTS THROUGH TEAMWORKING

The evidence of high-performing teams is around us all the time. Here are three examples:

1. Formula 1 racing teams are a clear example, with at least three key roles:
   - a star place for the individual driver
   - an operational team performing the changes as the vehicle comes in for service
   - behind the scenes a support team to provide the race strategy.
2. Soccer teams are often made up of outstanding individual performers but work together towards a common goal on the day of the match.
3. Organizations that realize their business objectives, business improvement and rapid growth, for example Powergen, using project teams to manage change since privatization.

Already perhaps there is a lesson to learn from the two sporting examples: what do they do that makes them different from other project teams? They spend 90 per cent of their time practising, rehearsing and developing their strategies and processes before they attempt the project. You may say that this is not possible to do in business, construction or Information Technology (IT), but there is a school of thought that says 'We don't know what we are capable of until we try!'

PRACTICAL GUIDELINES

PURPOSE

The amazing thing is that in the case of emergency we experience the ideal characteristics of teamwork – a willingness to get involved, to take any role, to work cooperatively together, all driven by a desire to rescue and to save others from pain or disaster. It is this power of purpose that seems to provide the direction, resource strategy and key roles of the team, often to great effect. So how can this principle be applied to every project? This is the first most important task for the project leader:

- To define the purpose of the project, clarify the definition with the client, and then share that purpose with the project team.

It sounds easy of course. Unfortunately, very often the client cannot articulate the purpose and this is the time when the project leader needs courage to explore and to challenge the client for measured definition. In addition, it is the time to involve other key team members in seeking additional clarification from their professional counterparts in the client's organization. This is the first collective team task.

Having sought clarity of definition and tested the interpretation with all of the key players now is the time to go public; it is the achievement of the purpose of the project that must become the dominant driver. It is the power of purpose that will drive the project forward and enable the project team to perform through all adversity:

● The purpose acquires real power when it is made visible.

This should become the project vision (a drawing of the intended building, a map of the intended system, a group of people sharing the new hospital resources). In addition, a similar but enlarged picture should be placed about the project site, in the project office and with the client, consultants, suppliers and other key stakeholders. In addition, this 'picture' could become the progress map gradually making the transformation from the existing circumstance to the final vision as it is duly updated as the project progresses. (This focuses the attention of the stakeholders on the success criteria (Turner 2000).) It is the purpose that provides the 'meaning of life' for the period of the project and so enables project team members to identify a framework within which to determine their three most important needs:

1. What is expected of me?
2. Where do I fit in?
3. How am I getting on?

When these fundamental requirements of purpose and personal needs are satisfied you might ask yourself, 'Do I need to spend time at all on team building?' The answer may well be no!

PROJECT TEAM SELECTION

If a group has cohesion, spirit and a sense of purpose, it can accomplish any project task, from installing a new IT system to raising money for the Red Cross. We believe that in order to achieve this magical balance you need to seriously consider the make-up of personalities in your prospective project team. Your reality may be that the team is composed of 'whoever is available at the time', hardly the way to select a team for the 'premier division', so fight this stance tooth and nail. One of the key merits of deciding to have a team is the possibility of a wide variety of talents and capabilities, so it is worth thinking about the nature of the project, the project needs and the characteristics of the other stakeholders who will need to be managed. The results of this examination will lead you to consider the best mix for the team; professional expertise is never enough. You might start by considering some of these key traits as essential requirements for your team:

- those who seek to accomplish the task
- those who will be concerned with the quality of working relationships
- those who strive for closure and control
- those who seek the ideal solution
- those who want to leap into action immediately
- those who would prefer to ponder on the option and think things through
- those who excel at detail and those who love the concepts and the possibilities.

Using a rugby analogy, the project leader is the scrum half, who hands off an assignment to a package leader (back row), who uses support staff (forwards) to move a project ahead to a final goal (the try line). In practical terms you need to select a team to match the demands of the project. Many projects require extroverts to sell the project to the client and the support units in their own project organization. Equally there is a need for different more imaginative personalities who will generate alternative means for raising the money, plus a balance of others who will pound the pavements and follow through on commitment plans.

It's worth compiling key criteria for your project and drawing up a balance card to ensure that you select those team players that bring the skill, knowledge and experience with the personality to match the demands of the project (Figure 5.1). Take time to interview potential team members who have been chosen for their functional expertise to determine how they fit with the management style, culture and demands of the project. These are some questions you might ask:

1. Tell me about the best project leader you've worked for.
2. Why was he or she a good leader?
3. What was your least favourite leader like?
4. How did you handle things you didn't like about him or her?
5. Tell me about a disagreement between you and a previous boss. How did you resolve it?
6. What actions are necessary to make a high performance project team?

If you were responsible for selecting a professional sports team then the elements would be clearly defined roles for team members, an explicit purpose uniting the team, an agreed game plan and a coach. So, in addition to thinking about the team selection, consider whom you will choose as your personal or team coach or mentor.

Project role	Technical or functional expertise	Personality profile (Problem-solving and decision-making capability)	Key project demands

Figure 5.1   Balance card for project team selection

CONDITIONS FOR TEAMWORKING

Perhaps the most basic conditions for good teamworking seem to be too obvious, but frequently they are not truly considered. They are size, purpose, goals, skills, approach and accountability. Paying rigorous attention to these is what creates the conditions necessary for team performance. Listening to successful teams you will find that they are committed to their purpose, goals and approach. Alongside these thoughts you need to acknowledge that we do not easily take responsibility for the performance of others, nor lightly let them assume responsibility for us. By applying rigorous attention to these performance requirements and conditions for teamworking most groups can deliver the goods.

FOCUSING ON TEAM BASICS

Katzenbach and Smith (1993) suggest that managers should focus on team performance and team basics issues (Figure 5.2). It is through disciplined action, much the same as following a diet, that true teams are born. They shape a common purpose, agree on performance goals, define a common working approach, develop high levels of complementary skills and hold themselves mutually accountable for results. Integrated with this basic approach real teams always find ways for each individual to contribute and gain distinction.

TEAM CHARTER

Team commitment might take the form of a team charter that sets out the common approach the team have adopted for themselves. The elements of such a charter could constitute the following:

● purpose of the project
● key performance goals
● project team values

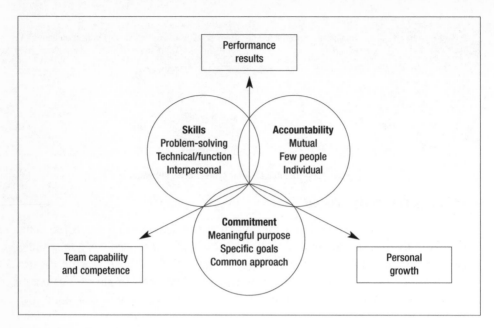

Figure 5.2   Focusing on team basics

- roles and responsibilities
- managing issues and conflict resolution
- assessment and team effectiveness.

The purpose

We have already mentioned that purpose will have the most significant influence on the progress of the project and therefore the team, the key word being *visibility*.

The key performance goals

The goals must be aligned with the project purpose and the organization-wide goals. The goals serve as benchmarks for which the project sponsor and each stakeholder group, those parties that have a vested interest in the team's success, will hold the team accountable. Some necessary groundwork will be required here to develop a clear understanding of the sponsor and stakeholder needs and expectations. The goals should be aligned to:

- organizational measures for return on investment and profits
- team qualitative and quantitative goals that measure the project outputs
- individual goals that measure the results of team members.

The goals are likely to reflect the critical success factors that have been agreed with the client. For a re-engineering project team the critical success factors might be cycle time, costs and customer service. Others might be revenue enhancement, market share gain and employee satisfaction. A matrix that identifies accountability for goals should be created (Figure 5.3). The goal leader must ensure that the goals, when translated into workable objectives, are SMART, maybe even SMARTIES (Figure 5.4).

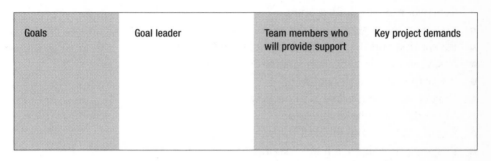

Goals	Goal leader	Team members who will provide support	Key project demands

Figure 5.3   Goal matrix

S	Specific
M	Measurable
A	Achievable
R	Realistic
T	Time bound
I	Involve the appropriate team members
E	Environmentally safe and acceptable
S	Success-oriented

Figure 5.4   SMART(IES) goals

Project team values

Goals define what we seek to achieve; our values indicate how we will 'behave' to achieve them. Establishing these ground rules of agreed team behaviour is vital to success. Often we discover what works by learning what does not work. Behaviour is so crucial to team success or failure that a willingness to abide by agreed values and norms should be a qualification for membership. Making that expectation non-negotiable sends a strong message. When people refuse to abide by expectations they are, in effect, deciding not to be on the team. Typically, values and norms evolve over time and often remain unspoken and unwritten unless they are violated. In practice there are some basic ground rules that can be defined at the outset:

- Share all relevant information.
- Focus on interest and not position.
- Be specific and use examples to illustrate the point.
- Disagree openly with other members of the team.
- Invite questions and comment.
- Expect all team members to participate.
- Make decisions by consensus.
- Explain the reasons behind the words.
- Respect and value each other's time.
- Conduct self-critique.

A significant influence will be the level of trust within the project team and this seems an appropriate place to suggest some ways of building it:

- Convey consistent principles.
- Give team members plausible explanations for actions.
- Offer status reports and forecasts.
- Make realistic commitments.
- Showcase what you know.
- Protect the interest of people who aren't present.
- Show compassion.
- Verify understanding.

Roles and responsibilities

The functional roles and responsibilities for the project should be clearly defined within the team with a balanced load spread between the players on an equal basis. In addition to the conventional expert functions there are a number of other key duties that will need to be fulfilled. Here are some examples:

1. *Customer/client service contact*   Who monitors the client's expectations?
2. *Liaison with head office*   Who builds collaboration?
3. *Mr or Ms Integrity*   Who provides the role model of behaviour?

4. *Community and interface developer* Who monitors how the project will impact on the community?
5. *Team motivator* Who provides that extra burst of enthusiasm when all are down?
6. *Challenger and supporter of the workforce* Who ensures that all views are taken into account?
7. *On-the-job educational developer* Who seeks out novel ways of keeping people informed and up to date?
8. *Crazy idea and innovation challenger* Who challenges conventional behaviour?
9. *Fun generator and celebration king/queen* Who generates celebration and makes sure that the team honour individual and group accomplishments?

Managing issues and conflict resolution

Managing project team issues should constitute a regular feature in the weekly review programme. One process that works effectively has five stages:

1. Ask team members to identify, without comment, the issues the team need to address. List these issues on a flip chart without any attempt to order or prioritize. Typically they will relate to team issues to do with procedures, practices, project strategy or roles and responsibilities, and sometimes morale and commitment.
2. Agree with the team the issues that should be challenged. There may be some that can be resolved very quickly, for example when information is needed. Prioritize the remainder and decide how many can be adequately examined in the permitted time.
3. Give the individual team member who raised the issue the opportunity to present it in more detail and give the other members the opportunity to ask questions for clarity. This part of the process often requires strong direction to ensure that the focus remains on clarification and not solution generation.
4. Ask the issue presenter to affirm the definition of the issue; sometimes it might have changed out of all recognition from the original statement.
5. Ask the other team members, in turn, to present their idea of a solution to the revised issue. The project leader will then have the task of deciding if further discussion and consensus agreement is necessary if the issue has wider implications.

With teams of independent, diverse thinkers, it is inevitable that differences will arise (see Chapter 8). Establishing the ground rules as we have indicated will help. In addition it pays to agree on a process for managing conflict and identifying trained facilitators who can support positive conflict resolution:

1. Establish ground rules on how to manage one-on-one and team conflict.
2. Adopt a step-by-step model for conflict resolution based on:
   - questioning the situation
   - identifying the problem
   - determining the implications of the problem
   - identifying the needs
   - developing alternative forms of resolution to meet the needs
   - evaluating the alternatives against the needs to determine the best choice
   - generating appropriate action plans.

On occasions you might deliberately encourage dispute or productive conflict – it can lead to magic when team members express their opinions, no matter how disagreeable they may seem. More ideas are put on the table, which can lead to more discovery, which can lead to quantum leaps in improvement and innovation. Agree on an internal or external third-party facilitator whom the team will use to assist them with more complex conflict.

Assessment and team effectiveness

An important feature of team development is team effectiveness, and measuring the 'well-being' of a team is one way of determining team progress. Figure 5.5 gives a structure which works well and is recommended for use from the start of a project and conducted on a regular basis during the initial months. The model identifies seven key measures of team success and asks individual team members to make their own judgement against each measure before then sharing their results with the other members of the team. It is then up to the team to discuss any differences and to seek to find understanding and ways to resolve them.

FURTHER OPPORTUNITIES FOR GROWTH

THE THIRD COMPETENCE

Why is it that some project teams have succeeded where others have not? The answer could lie in another aspect of individual difference, that is the basic assumptions that we bring with us to every project problem and decision (see Chapters 9 and 10).

- One way of avoiding this trap is to think of yourself as an immigrant. Then you

Item	1	2	3	4	5	6
Purpose – the team members understand the purpose and commit their energy to achieving it.						
Role – all the team members have a common understanding of the team's role						
Strategy – the team members understand the team's strategy and use it to guide their day-to-day activities						
Processes – the team's processes are optimal for its role and purpose						
People – the team members feel well utilized and valued						
Feedback – the team constructively uses the feedback it receives						
Interfaces – the team's key relationships with others are productive						

Figure 5.5   Audit of team effectiveness

are not hung up with what you believe the rules to be and you make no assumptions as to what is possible or not.

Perhaps these are some of your assumptions:

- I can't speak directly to the client.
- The suppliers are looking for ways to rip us off.
- The project team members are not willing to give it what it takes.
- Doing it the way I've always done it is the best way.
- People are not willing to change.
- I know my boss's goals.

The truth is that very often people have not been asked to contribute, they would be willing to change if you showed them how to and the suppliers are looking for continuity and would be happy to join your 'think tank' if you asked them. You do it your way because it's comfortable not because it's the best.

COMMUNICATION

'Guys, we're in this together!' How often do you hear this? A plea when the walls seem to be finally caving in or a rallying cry to keep the team focused? To quote experience on a large engineering contract:

There was always a lot of disagreement, different ideas, different areas of emphasis. But there was always self-respect and respect for others.

So what constitutes enough sharing and communication? Here's one example:

- meetings as a team every morning from 08.00 to 08.20
- a meeting each week to review the progress, performance and process of relationships on the project – for a *maximum* of two hours
- a shared lunch break on Wednesdays in the project leader's office, simple buffet lunch, open house meeting to which all are invited, including key suppliers and support staff from the parent organization; no minutes taken, but mountains of information exchanged
- when issues cannot be resolved at the weekly meetings, the full team gathers at the project leader's home on Sunday; they demand candour and objectivity.

The outcome of these practices was a fanatical belief in what the team were trying to achieve, which had a significant impact on each individual as well as the parent organization. They really believed they would make a difference. Some other ideas that come to mind:

- humour board for jokes and stories
- regular 'snapshots' of the team at work and play
- going to the cinema, theatre, sports game together
- continuing to seek novel ways of sharing and developing understanding.

CREATING YOUR OWN REALITY

Every project offers the project team members the opportunity to create their own new reality. An example of this is Russian Olympian Vasily Alexeev. He was trying to break a weight-lifting record of 500 pounds. He had lifted 499 but couldn't, for the life of him, lift 500. Finally his trainers put 501.5 pounds on the bar and rigged it so it looked like 499 pounds. Of course, you can guess the result: he lifted it easily. Once he had created this new reality, other lifters went on to break his record. Why? Because they now knew it was possible to lift 500 pounds. The British athlete who broke a similar barrier was Roger Bannister when he became the first man to run the mile in under 4 minutes and as a consequence many others followed. The limits we set ourselves exist in our mind. Sometimes if we let our hearts do the talking and believe in our ability to overcome perceptions, we can create another reality. Just imagine the possibilities when the project team truly believe in the purpose.

TEAM DECISION-MAKING

Team members bring unique experience, knowledge and skill to a team and very often cultural and language differences, an international construction team for example, and sometimes in these circumstances of multi-nationality, decision-making can become extremely onerous. One approach to this is the Delphi technique. It consists of collecting successive (usually two or three) rounds of inputs from team members, submitted without consultation between them. As each round is completed, individual inputs are consolidated and circulated back to the members for review before they provide the next input. Thus individuals see consensus developing, but without knowing who is adopting a given position, and without the potential biasing effect of face-to-face interaction. The resulting decision should reflect a position everyone can live with. This approach is particularly useful when contentious issues have to be resolved, or when you need to minimize the likelihood that, because of their style or personality, certain individuals will have an undue influence on the team's decision.

TEAM GROWTH AND DEVELOPMENT

This classic model for the journey that teams experience together seems to hold good:

- Forming – competent individuals
- Storming – competitive individuals
- Norming – competent team
- Performing – achieving team
- Mourning – appreciating team.

This model provides a frame of reference for judging the growth and strength of the teamworking process and warrants periodic evaluation on the agenda at the project review meetings. The questions to ask might include the following:

1. At what stage of the model are we at the moment?
2. How does that fit with the project life cycle?
3. What actions are being taken to move the team to the next stage?
4. What are we learning from our collective experience?
5. How are we sharing that knowledge with other project teams?

If you were in the theatre you would find all of the elements of project team building, plus more. There would be the common goals, defined roles, interdependence, firm deadlines, coaching and feedback. The uniqueness in this list is coaching, a responsibility of every leader. In the theatre you would experience the greatest degree of coaching during rehearsal, perhaps the secret weapon of the most astute project leader. Consider when rehearsal could truly add value:

- pre-commencement period
- testing understanding of goals
- potential problem analysis
- risk analysis
- presentation and meeting the media
- project completion.

And working and learning together to develop the team and personal skills in:

- process improvement techniques
- problem-solving
- group-conflict management
- interactive skills
- consensus and compromise
- process methodologies.

The team must learn to find their own solutions, they must realize that they are in control and that no one else is going to tell them what to do or how to do it. The team shares authority, and decision-making; ideally there should be no team bosses – only leaders and facilitators.

PERSONAL DEVELOPMENT

A starting point is to introduce individual self-assessment as a process to identify personal attributes to be developed through the project. This process can be further reinforced in the following ways:

1. Ask each team member to assess privately his/her own contributions to the team.
2. Discuss how to encourage/support increased contributions from all members.
3. Brainstorm how to make members feel more included, confident or engaged.

To learn by experience, one has to experience, then reflect on that experience to extract the learning. Learning boards can be located adjacent to or within the project environment to encourage project team members to share their learning experiences: perhaps a database can be introduced to build a knowledge base related to the project. Personal development is primarily the responsibility of the individual. In this age of rapid change, skills can become obsolete overnight. You have to keep pushing the envelope of your own experience and competence if you hope to keep up with the evolving needs of your job and profession. Perhaps these few practical tips can help your capacity to stay ahead of change:

1. Learn to be a better listener – 'You don't learn when you're talking.'
2. Read professional journals and business magazines from different industries – once a week take time out to find two new things that relate to your project.
3. Let your children tutor you – they know more than you about a lot of subjects.
4. Volunteer – in most voluntary activities everyone is the same. It changes your perspective on hierarchy and authority.
5. Read what has stood the test of time – Aristotle, Shakespeare, Adam Smith.

QUICK WINS

Developing high-quality project teams is as much about public profile as it is about output and performance. Acknowledging the team members at an early stage can establish a commitment that will have endurance. What are some of the possibilities?

- Establish a project team base with its own identity on the door.
- Develop a challenging identity, logo or name to add character to the team.
- Select an identity that in some way characterizes the nature of the project. For example is it about speed of completion, high image or quality, innovative or original?
- Turn the logo into a lapel badge, a car sticker or attach it to documentation to share with other project partners.
- Involve people at the pre-commencement stage so they can contribute to project strategy.
- Meet other stakeholders such as the client, in-house support teams, suppliers, investors, local community influencers, statutory services that have some assessment function.
- Involve in-house or outside press agents as part of the project marketing machinery.
- Ensure that basic resources are quickly on board so that individuals can make an immediate contribution on their arrival.
- Start a cartoon board.
- Create an information board giving three vital pieces of information (Figure 5.6). There may be several boards located about the site, of a size to ensure the best visibility.

New members	Project purpose	Member achievements
A welcome to new members of the team (individuals or other companies), with a definition of how they will be contributing, some personal history and a photograph	A picture of how the project will be when completed Or a before progress framework (bar chart) and expected result	An acknowledgement As the project progresses this panel might be a grateful 'thank you' to the departing member Or it could be an opportunity to feature the contribution and performance of a member

Figure 5.6   Project information board

TEAM LEADERSHIP

The project team leader today carries many roles; those of team facilitator, coach, mentor, as well as leader are the most apparent (see Chapter 6). Experience says that many project leaders survive by accident rather than design, perhaps the case for many organizations. Surviving by design means starting by taking stock of all stakeholders who have an interest in your project and determining who has influence and how they will benefit from the project, and don't forget the hidden stakeholders – people who may have personal reasons for not wanting this initiative of yours. Your analysis will reveal a surprising number of players: rate them as positive (supportive) or negative (resistant) and ask yourself these key questions about each of them:

1. What do you want of them as a stakeholder: to provide funding, lend their name to the project?
2. Consider the stakeholder's goals, values and needs.
3. Consider what concerns he or she might have that would cause resistance.
4. Determine what actions could address these concerns.
5. Consider the stakeholder's possible objections. How will you respond?
6. Determine the approach that is likely to work the best with this person – fact-based, value-based, participative or collaborative?

Again, the role is similar to that of an orchestral conductor, allowing each talented individual to have his or her moment of distinction, to cultivate the team spirit of each group in the orchestra and similarly allowing them their moment while maintaining a direction and symbiosis that presents a complete and whole picture.

REFERENCES AND FURTHER READING

Briner, W., Hastings, C. and Geddes, M. (1993), *Project Leadership*, 2nd edition, Gower, Aldershot.

Katzenbach, J. R. and Smith, D. K. (1993), *The Wisdom of Teams*, Harvard Business School Press, Cambridge, MA.

Turner, J. R. (2000), 'Project success and strategy', in J. R. Turner and S. J. Simister (eds), *The Gower Handbook of Project Management*, Gower, Aldershot.

6 Managing and leading

David Partington

What makes an effective leader? Are leaders born or can they be taught? To what extent does the effectiveness of a leader depend on the specific situation? How does leading differ from managing? What do effective managers and leaders do? Attempts to answer questions such as these have made the subject of leadership of central interest to managers and social scientists since the beginning of the formal study of management. The reason for this is the obvious link, in theory and in practice, between leadership effectiveness and business success.

In addition to its general importance to the business world, leadership has a special significance for project managers. One reason for this is that notions of leadership are central to that most fundamental project management principle – the project manager as single, integrative source of responsibility. Very small project groups – those with fewer than seven or eight members – can sometimes function without a leader, either one who is formally designated or one who emerges naturally. In all but the smallest groups, however, the operation of some sort of formal or informal leadership hierarchy is inevitable, and is necessary for the group to achieve its goals.

For some, the titles 'project leader' and 'project manager' are synonymous. Indeed, from the viewpoint of many people in organizations, leadership and management are indistinguishable. But another reason why leadership is taking on a new importance for many project managers lies in an emerging key difference between leadership and management, especially in the context of the implementation of planned change in organizations. (Rodney Turner addresses this point (Turner *et al.* 1996, Chapter 6) and concludes, by comparison with well known politicians, that management and leadership are different.) A comparison of traditional definitions of leadership with more recent ideas illustrates this difference. Defining for managerial purposes a word that is in common everyday usage is never straightforward. In common with words like power, control and politics, leadership is a potent word which has different meanings for different people. However, most traditional meanings combine three common elements, emphasized in the following definition:

> Leadership is the ability to *influence* the activities of a *group* of followers in their efforts to set and achieve *goals*.

This defines *transactional* leadership: the influence of a group of followers in the pursuit of defined, rational goals. This influence is normally achieved through the explicit or implicit offer of some form of reward, which may not always be wholly, or even partly, financial.

Theories of transactional leadership focus on the job of the leader as clarifier of role and task requirements, and as monitor and rewarder of task-related activity. Using definitions of transactional leadership like the one above, there is little to distinguish leadership from management, since most traditional and widely cited attempts to define management have tended to emphasize similar transactional roles. Fayol (1950), for example, defined the five roles of the manager as commanding, organizing, planning, controlling and implementing. Although some of Fayol's terms today sound unfashionably bureaucratic and militaristic they nevertheless present a strong parallel to the essential elements of transactional leadership. Mintzberg also emphasized the rational side of leadership, although in less belligerent fashion, defining the role in terms of eight skills: communication skills, information skills, people management skills, disturbance-handling skills, decision-making skills, resource allocation skills, entrepreneurial skills and reflecting (that is, planning) skills.

In contrast with these traditional ideas of leadership and management, more recent perspectives of leadership tend to emphasize the *transformational* role of the leader in bringing about change. Transformational leaders 'change the way people think about what is desirable, possible and necessary' (Zaleznik 1977). Transformational leadership has a distinctive orientation towards identity, purpose and change. This subtle alteration in meaning not only sets leadership apart from the relatively ordinary concerns of day-to-day management, but also underlines why the concept of leadership is of special importance to project managers. Increasingly project managers are concerned not only with setting and pursuing goals, but also with managing meaning and changing the way people think as part of the complex influencing process inherent in project leadership.

This chapter examines the main strands of transactional and transformational leadership theory and discusses their implications for project management professionals.

THEORIES OF LEADERSHIP

In pursuit of the holy grail of managerial performance there have been many attempts to distil the essence of effective leadership and to communicate that essence as information. The underlying idea is that this information can be absorbed and applied by anyone who is interested in becoming a leader or in appointing people to positions of leadership. Things are never that simple. Like all fundamental human issues, leadership reveals itself to be complex and multi-faceted. Attempts to pin it down have proved difficult and have led to conflicting answers. Indeed, few management concepts have incited as much controversy. Consider this quotation, attributed to Confucius:

Of bad leaders, the followers say, 'They were bad leaders.'
Of good leaders, the followers say, 'They were good leaders.'
Of the best leaders, the followers say, 'We did it ourselves.'

This presents the view, currently popular in management thinking, that effective leadership comes from the involvement, participation and empowerment of followers. The notion of employee empowerment is associated with many positive modern ideas of management and leadership, including the flattening of hierarchies, the project team approach, employee productivity and satisfaction, and the harnessing of individual creativity to the pursuit of organizational goals. However, experience shows that attempts at employee empowerment can have negative outcomes, including lack of direction, alienation, overwork and stress.

This reveals the other side of the leadership coin to that suggested by the quote. On the one hand, few would disagree that leadership is participation. On the other hand, one may argue equally credibly and forcefully that leadership is accountability and creating structured responsibility within a body of rules. Further, one may argue that leadership is *doing*.

So how can managers and leaders create appropriately structured conditions in which they and their followers can perform to the best of their abilities? There are four main schools of thought, or approaches, to the study of leadership:

1. The trait approach
2. The behavioural approach
3. The contingency approach
4. The visionary approach.

Each of the four has its own research tradition, its own underlying assumptions and its own purposes. An overview of the four approaches follows, with a discussion of some of their principal ideas in relation to project management.

THE TRAIT APPROACH

The idea behind the trait approach to leadership research and theory is that effective leaders share the same inherent personal qualities and characteristics. The trait approach thus assumes that leaders are born, not made. The purpose of trait theories is the *selection* of leaders, by matching supposedly desirable generic traits to the traits of individuals. Attempts to identify and isolate leader traits have focused on three main areas:

1. Abilities, for example communication skills and technical know-how
2. Personality variables such as self-confidence and introversion/extroversion
3. Physical traits, including size and appearance.

The trait approach was prominent until the late 1940s. Although it has been challenged and supplemented by later ideas, it still attracts significant attention and is currently enjoying revival in the study of new approaches to leadership (see the *visionary* approach).

Researchers, mostly psychologists, have been concerned with identifying the common traits of leaders who have proved to be effective, by comparison with non-leaders. This is a tall order, since a cursory examination of the traits of a selection of well-known contemporary leaders such as Tony Blair, the Pope and Bill Gates shows that they are individuals with very different characteristics. Nevertheless, trait research has produced some valid findings. For example, one relatively recent study of the characteristics of real-life successful leaders found six consistent leadership traits (Kirkpatrick and Locke 1991). These six traits and their implications for project managers are discussed below.

1. DRIVE AND AMBITION

Effective leaders are ambitious in their work and careers. The possession of drive is clearly an important attribute for project managers, since the success of many projects depends on the relentless, energetic and focused pursuit of difficult goals, in highly uncertain and volatile circumstances. Personal ambition is a significant characteristic of project managers. Anne Keegan and Rodney Turner (Chapter 4) report that when they asked a senior project director how his firm identified those 25 year olds who would make good project managers and directors in twenty years' time, he said: 'Those who are vocal with their ambitions.'

Most people who move into project management take a bold step away from the relative security of a line or technical function. Unlike some jobs where it is relatively easy, in the short term at least, to rest on one's laurels, project managers' ambition must be sustained. Establishing and maintaining career success in project management hinges on the highly visible outcomes of a manager's recent project assignments.

2. THE DESIRE TO LEAD AND INFLUENCE OTHERS

Effective leaders have a strong desire to lead and influence others. For project managers, such a desire is essential, since a key, defining role of a project manager is exerting influence in many ways, at many levels and in many directions. Good project managers have a strong ability to lead and motivate their team. They must also be skilled at building a winning relationship with their clients, ensuring the right level of senior management and external support for the project and getting the best from technical managers and specialist experts. To be able to lead and influence others, good leaders must be good communicators. Anne Keegan and Rodney Turner (Chapter 1 and 4) report a project director who said that the essence of good leadership was to be able to 'Communicate the goal; communicate the process.'

3. HONESTY AND INTEGRITY

Effective leaders exhibit above average levels of honesty and integrity. Unlike some other important leadership traits, these are widely perceived as desirable and valued personal attributes in their own right. Their opposites, dishonesty and lack of integrity, oppose society's norms of acceptable behaviour. Because of the pioneering, multi-agency nature of many projects, there are frequent opportunities for the project manager purposefully to mislead factions who are associated less centrally with the project and its information processes, or to manipulate situations for personal advantage. Good project managers know that they are under the spotlight and that any benefits of less than total honesty and integrity will be short-lived at best.

4. SELF-CONFIDENCE

Effective leaders have a belief in their own abilities that goes with feeling in control of change. As a result, they are more likely to actively seek information, to act confidently and decisively on the basis of information which may necessarily be incomplete and to have the courage to change course if necessary. All of these behavioural attributes find strong resonance with the project manager's role.

5. INTELLIGENCE

Effective leaders tend to have above average intelligence and problem-solving ability. Project managers are faced with a constant need to find creative solutions to unprecedented problems, both managerial and technical. Their superior intelligence is often revealed by their unusual ability for breadth and depth of thinking.

6. TECHNICAL KNOWLEDGE

Effective leaders usually have in-depth technical knowledge of their area of responsibility. Some observers have claimed that project management is a generic ability, and that good project managers are able to apply their skills to any project, regardless of technology. To a limited extent this is true, since the unique quality of many projects will embody at least some element of technical novelty which must be learned or discovered. Indeed, there is some evidence of transferability of successful project managers from one industrial context to another. Nevertheless, few successful project managers would argue against the obvious benefits of possessing adequate technical knowledge relating to their project.

The shortcomings of the trait approach lie in its search for a common set of traits possessed by all leaders, regardless of what they are leading. The personal qualities needed to lead a nation, a religious order or a multinational corporation are clearly different. In the field of project management it is easy to argue that different project leadership characteristics are required at different phases in a single project, let alone from one project to another.

THE BEHAVIOURAL APPROACH

The second school of thought about what makes an effective leader, the behavioural approach, signalled a move away from the trait approach. For a period of twenty years, starting in the late 1940s, the focus of attention turned towards the preferred behavioural styles of effective leaders.

The basic premise underlying the behavioural approach is that effective leaders behave in the same ways. Research has been aimed at identifying the behavioural styles of effective leaders. Do they tend to use a more democratic style or are they more autocratic? A number of studies of behavioural styles were carried out between the late 1940s and the late 1960s. Using subordinates' descriptions of the behaviour of leaders, including both successful and unsuccessful leaders, the studies attempted to identify the principal dimensions of leadership behaviour and to relate these to measures of performance. The broad finding was that much of leadership behaviour could be distilled and expressed on two dimensions, broadly relating to *task* and *people*. The dimensions are given variety of different labels; typical are the two axes of the Blake and Mouton (1964) 'managerial grid'. Blake and Mouton's two dimensions, scored on the grid from 1 to 9, are:

1. *Concern for production* Leaders with a strong concern for production emphasize technical and task aspects of work, including the organizing of work, work relationships and goals.
2. *Concern for people* Leaders who are strong on this dimension emphasize interpersonal relationships and consideration for subordinates' needs.

Using the grid, managers are rated according to the concerns which dominate their particular style in their pursuit of results. Their combined rating on the two dimensions expresses their behavioural style. The extreme styles are labelled and described by Blake and Mouton as follows:

- 1,1 Impoverished management (low concern for production; low concern for people): Exertion of minimum effort to get required work done is appropriate to sustain organization membership.
- 9,1 Authority-obedience (high concern for production; low concern for people): Efficiency in operations results from arranging conditions of work in such a way that human elements interfere to a minimum degree.
- 1,9 Country club management (low concern for production; high concern for people): Thoughtful attention to needs of people for satisfying relationships leads to a comfortable, friendly organization atmosphere and work tempo.
- 9,9 Team management (high concern for production; high concern for people): Work accomplishment is from committed people; interdependence through a 'common stake' in organization purpose leads to relationships of trust and respect.

Unlike the trait approach, which assumes leaders are born not made, the underlying rationale of the behavioural approach is that leadership behaviour can be learned. The purpose of behavioural theories is teaching people how to change the assumptions that control their behaviour in order to become more effective leaders. Blake and Mouton concluded the best performance was obtained by managers who scored high on both dimensions (a 9,9 style).

The clear implication of behavioural leadership theories for project managers is that they must possess both 'hard' and 'soft' project management skills, since neglecting either will result in sub-optimal project performance. This hard versus soft dichotomy is well known to experienced project managers. Although the majority of basic project management textbooks concentrate on the 'hard' tools and techniques for planning and controlling cost, schedule and quality, the writers are usually at pains to point out the need for attention to the more elusive, 'soft' side of managing projects.

Like the pure trait approach, the simple behavioural approach suffers from problems of over-simplification, and the one-size-fits-all approach. We all know that different styles are often appropriate in different circumstances. These shortcomings were addressed in the next stage in the story of the study of leadership effectiveness, the contingency approach, which dominated the leadership research arena from the late 1960s to the early 1980s.

THE CONTINGENCY APPROACH

Towards the end of the 1960s there was a growing tendency for management theorists in general to move away from universal theories which would apply in every situation towards 'contingency' theories, based on the idea that 'it depends'. In the area of leadership effectiveness, as it became apparent that neither trait theories nor behavioural theories would work in every set of circumstances, the search was on for situational variables which moderated the effectiveness of different leader characteristics or behaviours. The contingency approach focuses on isolating critical situational influences on leadership success, for example the clarity of the task, the degree of conflict in the group or the culture of the organization. Several important contingency theories of leadership effectiveness have been developed, some more complex than others. Although the various theories differ in their underlying assumptions regarding what is important about leaders' characteristics and situational variables, the way in which these contingency approaches are applied tends to follow the same pattern:

1. Assess the characteristics of the leader.
2. Evaluate the situation in terms of key contingency variables.
3. Seek a match between the leader and the situation.

One contingency theory of leadership which is currently the subject of a lot of interest, and which has important implications for the project environment, is the path–goal theory (House 1971). The theory is based on the idea that the role of the leader is to provide support and/or direction in providing a *path* which will help the followers to achieve their *goals*, at the same time ensuring that these match the goals of the group's task. Following the three steps listed above, the path–goal theory works as follows.

Assess the characteristics of the leader

Path–goal theory identifies four leadership behaviours which contribute to the satisfaction and motivation of subordinates. Any combination of these may be exhibited, depending on the situation.

● Directive leaders define tasks, schedules and processes.
● Supportive leaders are friendly and concerned for followers' needs.
● Participative leaders involve followers in decisions.
● Achievement-oriented leaders set challenging goals and expect high performance.

Evaluate the situation in terms of key contingency variables

Path–goal theory has two classes of contingency factors which affect the relationship between leader behaviour and performance:

1. Environmental contingency factors:
   ● task structure
   ● formal authority system
   ● work group.
2. Subordinate contingency factors:
   ● locus of control (the extent to which people feel that they control their own destiny)
   ● experience
   ● perceived ability.

Seek a match between the leader and the situation

In path–goal theory, leader behaviour should be congruent with both environmental and subordinate contingency variables. Robbins (1997) lists eight ways in which path–goal theory works, which have tended to be supported by empirical evidence. These are described below, with examples of their implications for project managers.

1. Directive leadership leads to greater satisfaction when tasks are ambiguous or stressful than when they are highly structured and well laid out. When a project has the combined characteristics of high uncertainty and high importance, for example in the early stages of a key development initiative, more direction and guidance will be welcomed by subordinates.

2. Supportive leadership results in high employee performance and satisfaction when subordinates are performing structured tasks. On projects which involve the routine application of established processes, for example in the later, detailed stages of engineering projects, subordinates will appreciate and be motivated by a friendly, caring leader.

3. Directive leadership is likely to be redundant among subordinates with high ability or with considerable experience. Project managers who over-emphasize cost, schedule and quality objectives to self-believing experts will be wasting their time.

4. The clearer and more bureaucratic the formal authority relationships, the more leaders should exhibit supportive behaviour and de-emphasize directive behaviour. Effective project managers with a high degree of formal authority acting within a highly proceduralized environment, for example on longer-term public sector projects, should have less need to emphasize a style of direction and guidance and more need to counter the possible alienating effects of bureaucracy by adopting a sympathetic approach.

5. Directive leadership will lead to higher employee satisfaction when there is substantive conflict within a work group. Conflict is often unavoidable, and under certain conditions may be beneficial to the project by avoiding apathy and keeping the team alive and creative. Whether conflict is functional or dysfunctional to the project, however, it will be less a source of dissatisfaction to individuals if the project manager exhibits directive behaviour.

6. Subordinates with an internal locus of control (those who believe they control their own destiny) will be most satisfied with a participative style. People who naturally feel in control of their world will find project managers who seek appropriate involvement in project decisions more agreeable as leaders.

7. Subordinates with an external locus of control (those who believe they have little control over their own destiny) will be most satisfied with a directive style. People who generally feel powerless over their environment will have a tendency to resign their futures to fate, and to avoid seeking out information for improved decision-making. They will derive satisfaction from project managers who let them know what is expected of them.

8. Achievement-oriented leadership will increase subordinates' expectations that effort leads to high performance when tasks are ambiguously structured. The motivational effect of setting challenging goals will be heightened on projects which are executed in organizations with a dual power channel, such as the project/functional matrix in a project engineering firm or the management/clinician structure of a hospital.

One of the features of path-goal theory which makes it especially relevant to the project environment is its simultaneous focus on the needs of (i) the task, (ii) the team and (iii) the individual. There can be a tendency for inexperienced project managers to over-emphasize the first one or two of these and to make false assumptions about the alignment between the motivation and satisfaction of individuals and the project's objectives.

LEADER GENDER

Recently, much attention has been directed towards issues of gender in management and leadership, mostly in the form of debates and research on women in management. What is known about gender as a contingency factor in relation to leadership effectiveness? Studies show that the leadership styles of men have much in common with those of women. This is not surprising, given that those who occupy positions of formal leadership are both self-selected and selected by organizations on the basis of their self-confidence, intelligence, desire to lead and so on. But apart from the conclusion that similarities outweigh differences, it is apparent that women tend to employ a more participative leadership style, relying more on interpersonal skills such as negotiation and information-sharing to influence subordinates. Men tend to favour a more directive, command-and-control style, depending more on their formal authority. As the requisite styles of organizations and projects increasingly emphasize values of teamwork, participation, trust and cooperation, one may conclude that conditions for project leaders in many sectors are changing in favour of women.

THE VISIONARY APPROACH

We have seen how the ideas which influenced the study of leadership until the 1980s moved through three overlapping stages, represented here as the trait, behavioural and contingency approaches. The successive influence of each of these approaches has been one of emphasis rather than exclusivity, and today all three traditions live on in various forms, forever building on their origins and adapting to the changing conditions of society.

In the 1980s a new focus and approach to the study of leadership emerged. It became apparent that many successful organizations had been subject to the influence of a 'visionary' or 'charismatic' leader. Therefore, attention turned towards the identification of the personal abilities and characteristics of leaders who were clearly capable of a form of leadership which went beyond traditional ideas about the transactional role of the manager.

Transactional leadership, which emphasizes tasks, goals and performance, is limited by the explicit and implicit contracts between leader and followers. Visionary, 'transformational' leaders, on the other hand, are able to unite leader and followers in the pursuit of a higher purpose which transcends individuals' self-interest. Bryman (1996) illustrates the differences between these two conceptualizations of leadership, listing their components as follows:

1. Components of transactional leadership:
   - Contingent rewards: rewarding followers for meeting performance targets.
   - Management by exception: taking action mainly when task-related activity is not going to plan.
2. Components of transformational leadership:
   - Charisma: developing a vision, engendering pride, respect and trust.
   - Inspiration: motivating by creating high expectations, modelling appropriate behaviour, and using symbols to focus efforts.
   - Individual consideration: giving personal attention to followers, giving them respect and responsibility.
   - Intellectual stimulation: continually challenging followers with new ideas and approaches.

Most studies of visionary business leaders have been concerned with people in the highest positions of seniority, especially chief executives. However, experience shows that many attempts at bold organizational change which go beyond normal rational goals, and which depend on the articulation of an extraordinary vision of the future, are originated by leaders in less senior positions of formal authority. Many examples of visionary change arise from managers of important technology-related business improvement projects, where visions of the future are more immediate and problems with existing business processes are more apparent. Others occur in subsidiaries of multinationals or other dispersed organizations, when finding imaginative ways of surviving and dealing with present and expected future local conditions is more pressing than implementing the latest head office fad.

These kinds of change initiatives are usually dependent for their success on a high degree of senior management or head office support, or at least non-interference. However, when senior managers have little to gain personally from the success of a transformational change project, and often a lot to lose, this can be too much to expect. For these reasons successful attempts at radical change which are driven from the middle of organizations are likely to be difficult to sustain.

Despite these problems, efforts at initiating and leading organizational innovation from lower down the management ranks are becoming more common.

This is partly due to the increasing exposure to unsatisfactory aspects of the status quo which is experienced by managers of more routine internal projects of change. A common example of this phenomenon is the widespread perception at non-senior levels in many organizations of the need to establish a stronger culture of project management. Moving towards a project culture for dealing with change has become a pressing need for many organizations. It is often driven by project managers who have experienced frustration with barriers to change, which were caused by departmental hierarchies and perpetuated by senior management.

STAGES OF VISIONARY LEADERSHIP

There are four stages of visionary leadership. They represent clearly the distinctive life cycle of the kind of project or programme of change which, for an increasing number of people, has become a necessary feature of organizational life, and the new challenge for transformational project leaders.

1. The leader identifies the opportunity and the need for change, and formulates a vision of a future state that relates to those needs.
2. The leader communicates the vision, often by pointing out the unacceptability of the status quo.
3. The leader builds trust in the vision. The achievement of trust may be helped by building links with other powerful individuals and institutions with similar values or by showing followers what has been achieved by other organizations with related aims.
4. The leader leads by example and by empowering followers. Sometimes disempowering non-followers is also effective.

Some visionary leaders are better at forming and articulating visions than they are at implementing them, and some prominent visionaries have proved incapable of leading change successfully through the four stages. The following factors are those which commonly lead to failure in implementing transformational change:

1. *Moving at the wrong pace*   Problems can arise either from trying to achieve too much too quickly, resulting in change overload and intolerable employee stress, or from missing opportunities by not taking swift enough advantage of instability and dissatisfaction with the status quo.
2. *Inappropriate use of management consultants*   The right consultants can add value to a radical change initiative, especially in the early stages when the leader may need help and outside expertise in selling the need for change to those with the power to block it, and in formulating the detail. However, if the prolonged or excessive use of consultants makes them seem too central or

crucial to the change, the vision's underlying values can become distorted and followers may become disillusioned.

3. *Failure to put enough effort into communicating the opportunity and the need for change*   It is apparently too easy for leaders to forget or become distracted from the need for tireless efforts to communicate the vision of a better future. This is especially true in difficult times when general enthusiasm for the change is flagging.

4. *Inadequate scheduling*   Excessive formality and detail in planning and communicating change can be demotivating for followers who must own and implement the plans. On the other hand, leaders sometimes cause unnecessary confusion by avoiding scheduling the stages of the change. Sometimes this happens because leaders fear that formal plans may set them up for failure if the plans are not met. Another scheduling problem is tackling the easiest parts of the change first, whilst allowing the more intractable aspects to become even more entrenched.

5. *Inappropriate participation*   There is a trade-off between seeking too much involvement of followers in difficult decisions, especially when their advice is not used, and not allowing an appropriate level of involvement. The latter problem is especially likely to arise when one of the objects of the change is to establish a culture of increased participation.

CONCLUSIONS

This chapter has traced the evolution of ideas about business leadership effectiveness through four stages, labelled the trait approach, the behavioural approach, the contingency approach and the visionary approach. We have seen that all four approaches have important implications for project management. In particular, the growing emphasis on transformational leadership means that exerting influence by changing the way people think has become a valuable project leadership skill.

As for the future, it is possible to foresee that, more than ever, project managers will need to understand how to manage relationships in which they are not formally in command. Just as traditional views about the transactional role of the manager are becoming increasingly out of date, leading-edge ideas about project management are aligning with newer conceptions of leadership. The basis of the world economy is moving towards finite alliances, partnerships and contracts. The need to lead such relationships through their life cycle places effective project leadership skills at a premium.

REFERENCES AND FURTHER READING

Blake, R. R. and Mouton, J. S. (1964), *The Managerial Grid*, Gulf, Houston, TX.

Bryman, A. (1996), 'Leadership in organizations', in S. R. Clegg, C. Hardey and W. R. Nord (eds), *Handbook of Organization Studies*, Sage, London.

Fayol, H. (1950 [1916]), *Administration Industrielle et Générale*, Dunod, Paris.

House, R. J. (1971), 'A path–goal theory of leader effectiveness', *Administrative Science Quarterly*, September: 321–38.

Kirkpatrick, S. A. and Locke, E. A. (1991), 'Leadership: do traits matter?', *Academy of Management Executive*, May: 44–60.

Mintzberg, H. (1973), *The Nature of Managerial Work*, Prentice-Hall, Englewood Cliffs, NJ.

Robbins, S. P. (1997), *Essentials of Organizational Behaviour*, Prentice-Hall, Englewood Cliffs, NJ.

Turner, J. R., Grude, K. V. and Thurloway, L. (eds) (1996), *The Project Manager as Change Agent: Leadership, Influence and Negotiation*, McGraw-Hill, London.

Zaleznik, A. (1977), 'Managers and leaders: are they different?', *Harvard Business Review*, **55**: 67–78.

7 Managing stakeholders

Bill McElroy and Chris Mills

Regardless of how well you define and achieve the tangible deliverables of your project, failure to manage the project stakeholders adequately may cause your project to fail. This is not to say that project managers should disregard the need to satisfy the time, cost and performance objectives defined for their projects. Rather they should strive to achieve these objectives while also ensuring stakeholder satisfaction with the project and its outcome. This requires the project manager to view stakeholder satisfaction as a key project deliverable. As such, the project manager needs to be able to:

- identify stakeholders, and in particular key stakeholders
- define what will constitute satisfaction for each
- plan appropriate actions to ensure satisfaction
- monitor the effect of these actions
- be prepared to implement corrective actions if the desired outcome isn't being achieved.

To help the project manager achieve the above, this chapter attempts to explain why stakeholder management is important. It defines stakeholders, provides a framework for identifying key stakeholders and outlines how to 'manage' stakeholders.

DEFINITIONS

WHY IS STAKEHOLDER MANAGEMENT IMPORTANT?

Many of the factors which influence a project are not only external to it, but also often lie outside the sponsor organization. For example:

- change of government
- change of public opinion
- regulatory requirements
- economic performance – both within the sponsor organization and nationally
- change of business environment
- change of business direction
- competitor performance.

Because such factors are external to the project it could be argued that the project manager should simply ignore them as they will be a 'distraction'. But these distractions can have a major influence on whether a project will be a success. For example, based on recent experience, the cost of dealing with pressure groups protesting against a new bypass can add up to 15 per cent to the cost of the project. So effective project managers need to adopt a proactive approach. The key element of this is the identification of those who embody the external influences on the project (the project *stakeholders*), and managing the influence that they will bring to the benefit of the project (*stakeholder management*). This influence need not be detrimental to project success. Many stakeholders can assist the project manager by using contacts, trust and knowledge not available to the project team.

Stakeholder management is particularly important when dealing with 'soft' business-critical projects. In such projects the success criteria defined by the sponsor are often subjective, and any subversive efforts of the stakeholders will be less blatant than on projects with a high profile capital spend. An example of such criteria would be a desire to increase sales through a more 'proactive' response to customer enquiries. The achievement of such a goal would rely heavily on effective management of the project's stakeholders.

It was stated in the introduction to this chapter that the project manager should view stakeholder satisfaction as a key project deliverable. It should certainly be used as one of the measures of project success. However, as shown in Figure 7.1, whatever outcome is desired by individual stakeholders it will always be essential to safeguard support for future projects. The key point to remember is don't jeopardize future projects through poor relations now – effectively manage the project stakeholders not only to ensure success of the current project but also future ones as well!

WHO IS A STAKEHOLDER?

The term 'stakeholder' is a relatively recent introduction to the project management vocabulary. As such it is difficult to identify a definition which is widely used and accepted. In preparing this chapter reference was made to BS6079 (1996) *Guide to Project Management* which contains the following definition:

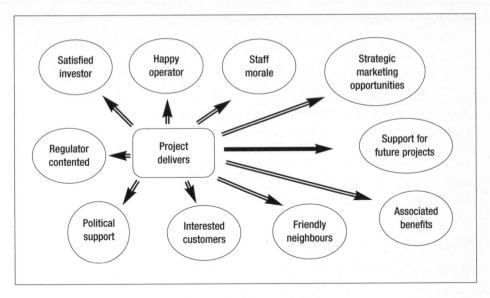

Figure 7.1   Stakeholder satisfaction

> A stakeholder is a person or group of people who have a vested interest in the success of an organisation and the environment within which the organisation operates.

In our view this definition, although robust, deals with stakeholders at too high a level. That is, it addresses organizational stakeholders rather than project stakeholders. It is therefore proposed that the BS6079 definition be slightly modified, as follows, to help identify stakeholders at a project level:

> A project stakeholder is a person or group of people who have a vested interest in the success of a project and the environment within which the project operates.

There is, however, a further problem with this definition. Potentially there will be lots of people and groups with a *vested interest* in your project and the environment within which it will operate. Stakeholders are everywhere! Stakeholders may have a vested interest because they are:

- investing in the project
- competitors
- competing for resources
- regulators
- affected by the project implementation
- affected by the project deliverables
- and so on.

Project managers therefore have to focus on those stakeholders who really

101

matter for their project. That is, they need to identify the key stakeholders. To clarify this, it is proposed that the definition above is expanded as follows:

> A key project stakeholder is a person or group of people who have a vested interest in the success of [the] project and the environment within which the project operates *and* who have an influence over its successful outcome.

Expanding on this definition, project managers have to focus on those individuals or groups who are interested and able to actually prevent or help them (influence) deliver a successful outcome for the project. This also reflects the fact that the vested interest of certain stakeholders may not always be a positive one – they could be interested in seeing the project fail rather than succeed. Key project stakeholders feature in the right-hand half of Figure 7.2.

WHAT IS STAKEHOLDER MANAGEMENT?

As with the term 'stakeholder' it is difficult to identify a common and widely used

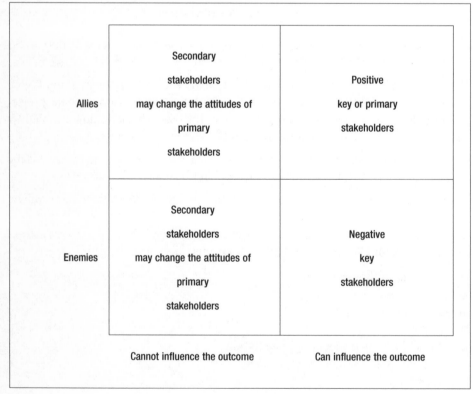

Figure 7.2   Stakeholder identification grid

definition for 'stakeholder management'. Again, when preparing this section reference was made to BS6079 and it was found that there was no definition given for stakeholder management. In the absence of this the following definition is proposed:

> Stakeholder management is the continuing development of relationships with stakeholders for the purpose of achieving a successful project outcome.

There are three key features of this definition. First, this is not a 'one-off' exercise (it continues throughout the project life cycle). Second, it is a two-way process (a relationship), not just telling stakeholders what you are going to do – you have to listen and negotiate as well. Third, stakeholders will make subjective assessments of project success. It is these assessments which will be remembered, long after compliance with the more objective success criteria of time, cost and performance have been forgotten.

THE STAKEHOLDER MANAGEMENT PROCESS

The stakeholder management process is illustrated in Figure 7.3. The key steps in this process are as follows.

IDENTIFY PROJECT SUCCESS CRITERIA

The project definition process should define the sponsor's success criteria in terms of time, cost and performance. Think beyond these, although they may be influenced by stakeholders. Consider those issues which are likely to affect or concern stakeholders directly. These are likely to be the softer issues surrounding the project, such as marketing, training or changes to working practices. Also, the environmental impact of construction projects, and associated project objectives to mitigate these, are increasingly attracting the interest of stakeholders.

IDENTIFY RESOURCE REQUIREMENTS

A project manager needs access to many resources to execute a project effectively. As shown in Figure 7.4 'resources' are not confined to tangible items such as materials and finance. They include intangible items such as support and emotion. The majority of these resources will not be under the direct control of the project manager, but are supplied by a stakeholder. As such, access to resources will be at the discretion of the stakeholder. This is relatively obvious

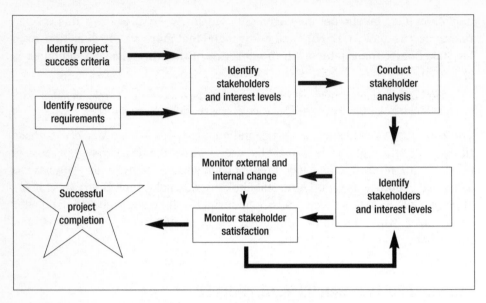

Figure 7.3   The stakeholder management process

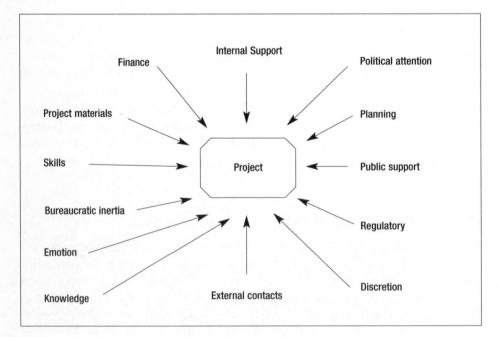

Figure 7.4   Stakeholder resources

when considering a stakeholder external to the organization undertaking the project. Some of these stakeholders can be bound by contract, although those supplying 'permissions' will be bound by statute and their decisions can be influenced by political expediency.

The availability of resources supplied by internal stakeholders should never be taken for granted, particularly in a matrix organization – the sponsor may well be committed to the project, but line managers might still be able to refuse to release key staff from operational responsibilities. For example, operator training may require the Operations Manager to identify trainees and make them available at the right time, but the Operations Manager might be always able to find more pressing issues to address in current operations.

This last example illustrates the importance of 'support' (internal and external) as a key resource provided by stakeholders. This relates both to their direct support (or opposition) for the project and to the support (or opposition) they can generate amongst other individuals and groups. As illustrated in Figure 7.5, stakeholders have a vital role to play as *change agents* – positively changing the way others view the project. As a general rule, the role of key stakeholders as change agents will be more crucial on soft projects. However, as indicated in Figure 7.5, the need for stakeholders to be incorporated as change agents is appropriate for both hard and soft projects. Examples of hard projects include:

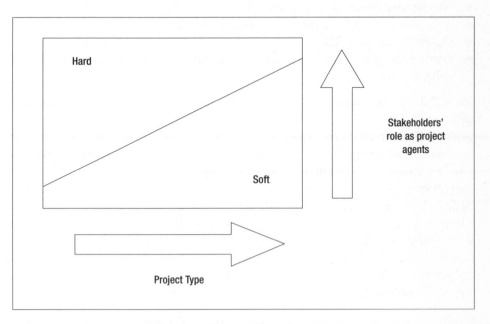

Figure 7.5   Stakeholders as change agents

- marketing a new road
- explaining how to get the best results from new plant
- getting users to think differently about software.

Examples of soft projects include:

- persuading people to change working practices
- getting staff to think differently about profit
- asking customers to purchase in new ways.

As has been said, and will be seen further below, it is naive to think that all stakeholders want to promote the change being delivered by the project. Also, there is a need to be clear on how the key project stakeholders will influence others and who will influence the key stakeholders.

IDENTIFY STAKEHOLDER GROUPS AND INTEREST LEVELS

Brainstorm a key stakeholder list from the following classes:

- Employees
- Senior management
- Customers (internal and external)
- Suppliers (internal and external)
- Neighbours (physical and within the supply chain)
- Resource providers (people, time, finance, consents)
- Government (local, UK, EU)
- Opinion formers (media, commentators, industry pundits, unions, internal departments).

Record these stakeholders on a register. An example of a stakeholder register is given in Figure 7.6. For each one, identify what, to them, constitutes a successful project. Their idea of project success may be totally different from yours or your sponsor's. For example, a landowner may have no interest in the benefits a pipeline across his land will bring to a community several miles away. His idea of project success will be to attract maximum compensation for the use of his land. Stakeholders' objectives may not always be obvious to the project manager or those close to delivery of the project and may need further research. When developing the key stakeholder list be certain to include 'secondary' stakeholders. These are stakeholders who do *not* have direct influence over the project, but who are able to change the attitudes of the key stakeholders ('primary' stakeholders).

Scheme: Rural sewerage scheme		Review date 24 Feb				Reviewers
Stakeholder name / group	Objectives	Awareness H/L	Support H/L	Influence H/L	Strategy	
Project Manager	Meeting project success criteria of time, cost, performance	H	H	H	Ensure company and line manager support	
Sponsor	Remove problem of failures and customer complaints Minimize disruption and compensation payments	H	H	H	Obtain active support. Keep informed of progress proactively	
Local residents	Minimal noise and mess As quick as possible No more flooding	H	L	H	Face-to-face contact, agree local contact, provision for compensation	
Local authority	Be informed	L	L	L	Involve from start, keep informed	
Environment Agency	Stop incidents, environmental improvements, close communication	H	H	H	Maintain close communication	
Woodland Trust (environmental pressure group)	No environmental detriment Early input to planning process	H	L	H	Early communication and involvement. Encourage relationship with Environment Agency	
Landowners	Maximum compensation for land take	H	L	H	Isolate by negotiating compensation and access details early. Document before and after positions very carefully	

Figure 7.6   An example of a stakeholder register

CONDUCT STAKEHOLDER ANALYSIS

Stakeholders' attitudes to the project will vary. They will range from:

- complete opposition (roads protesters, redundant internal employees), to
- complete support (landscaping industrial waste, new office building for staff).

The stakeholders' attitudes may also vary over time, particularly if the stakeholders are being exposed to effective management by the project team. The actions associated with this effective management need to be focused on the key stakeholders. But knowing who these are is not enough. The project team need to base their actions on the following:

- a refined assessment of the stakeholders' current attitude towards project success
- an awareness of the knowledge base on which the stakeholders' current attitude is based
- an understanding of the stakeholders' own objectives and how these can, if possible, be aligned with those of the project.

Guidance on mapping and analysis techniques to support the first two elements listed above are considered here. Steps taken to deal with the third element are outlined below.

The first step in the analysis is to assess the current level of support (or commitment) for the project amongst key stakeholders. But in order to provide information to guide effective stakeholder management this needs to be assessed against the commitment levels required to achieve success. This analysis can be produced as a matrix (Figure 7.7). The characteristics and behaviours of each level of commitment are:

- *Active opposition* Will not accept change as proposed by project. Will expend time and energy telling others the project is 'wrong', and will try to turn supporters against the project. Will withhold resources from the project, either overtly or covertly.
- *Passive opposition* Not happy with change as proposed by project, but will reluctantly accept it. When asked will voice opposition, but will not seek out opportunities to raise opposition to the project. Will provide resources to the project but may require coercing.
- *No commitment* Will accept change. Not opposed to or supportive of the project. Happy to see it proceed but not concerned if it succeeds or fails. Will provide resources, but only if it does not impact on their own operations.
- *Passive support* Wants change as proposed by project. When asked will voice

Stakeholders	Active opposition	Passive opposition	Not committed	Passive support	Active support
Suppliers			XO		
Executive directors				X	0 →
Staff	X		0 →		
National politicians				XO	
Finance Director				0	X ←
Local politicians		XO			

X = current position   0 = required position

Figure 7.7   Stakeholder commitment matrix

support, but will not seek out opportunities to gather support for the project. Will provide resources to project when asked, but may require prompting.

● *Active support*   Eager for change proposed by project. Will expend time and energy telling others the project is 'right' and will try to change opposers' views – without prompting from the project team. Will ensure that resources are available to the project as and when required.

There are a number of features to note from the figure:

1. Changing a stakeholder's commitment level will require effort by the project team. This will have to be balanced with all of the other activities the project team will need to carry out. Therefore the team should not be over ambitious about how far they can move stakeholders, particularly, as in the case of 'staff', if they are currently actively opposed. The team should focus on the key stakeholders, those with the most influence to affect the success of the project, and aim to achieve the minimum commitment level needed to ensure project success.

109

2. Where the stakeholders' current commitment matches their required commitment level (as in the case of 'suppliers') they must not be ignored. It is all too easy for ignored stakeholders to misinterpret the lack of communication from the project team as disinterest in their objectives. They may respond in a like fashion when required to deliver resources or support. Worse, they may be swayed by active opposers and change their attitude to the project as a result.

3. As in the case of the 'Finance Director' there can be stakeholders whose active support may actually have a disruptive effect on the project. This is often due to their active support raising or reinforcing negative attitudes in other key stakeholders.

4. The impact of stakeholder commitment on provision of resources to the project needs to be carefully considered by the project team when developing project plans. Where the analysis indicates resources may not be readily available, have contingency plans ready.

This commitment analysis will help to focus development of an appropriate strategy for managing each key stakeholder. A summary strategy can be entered on the Stakeholder Register, as shown in Figure 7.6. In developing these strategies it is worth remembering the definition of stakeholder management and, in particular, 'the need for the continuing development of relationships'. Therefore the strategies developed need to incorporate actions which will continue throughout the project life cycle and involve two-way communications.

These communications will be most effective if they are based on an awareness of the stakeholder's knowledge base. Stakeholders' commitment levels will, to a large extent, be based on their level of knowledge of the project. And based on this knowledge, stakeholders will make judgements of how the project will help, or hinder, them in meeting their own objectives. It is these judgements which will determine the stakeholders' satisfaction referred to in the introduction to this chapter. The stakeholders' level of knowledge will range from:

- *full awareness* they have gained knowledge of the project by detailed research, focusing on those aspects of the project which will help them meet their own objectives, to
- *total ignorance* they have gained knowledge of the project by hearsay not fact, and are therefore basing their attitudes towards the project on assumptions. Their decision on whether to increase their knowledge will depend on whether they believe they can use the project to further their own objectives.

These two attributes of stakeholders, commitment and knowledge, can be mapped on to a chart, such as that in Figure 7.8, to illustrate the knowledge base across the key stakeholders. To populate this chart plot each of the key stakeholders listed in Figure 7.6. Initially you will have to make certain assumptions regarding the knowledge base of each stakeholder. Be prepared to test these assumptions and revisit this chart throughout the project. There are a number of important points to note regarding where stakeholders lie on this chart:

1. *Quadrant 1 – Support/Aware* These supporters must not be taken for granted. In order to retain their support they need to be assured that the project will indeed help them meet their own objectives.
2. *Quadrant 2 – Support/Ignorant* This support is vulnerable and could easily be lost, particularly if the gaps in the stakeholder's knowledge base are filled by the views of opposers. The project team will therefore need to ensure that this support is protected and reinforced.
3. *Quadrant 3 – Oppose/Ignorant* This is a key target area for the project team, especially if the commitment mapping (Figure 7.7) indicates that there are stakeholders in this quadrant whose commitment needs to be increased. This chart suggests that it may be possible to achieve greater commitment by filling the gap in the stakeholder's knowledge base with positive messages regarding the project.
4. *Quadrant 4 – Oppose/Aware* These will be the most difficult stakeholders to

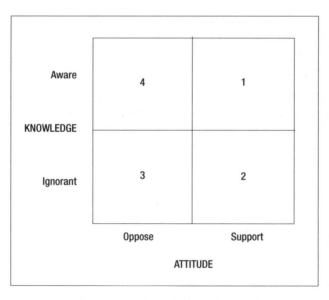

Figure 7.8   Plotting stakeholder knowledge base

manage. Indeed, as they are already aware, and are basing their opposition on this, it may never be possible to move them to support the project.

DEVELOP STRATEGY FOR EACH STAKEHOLDER

The analysis outlined in the previous section focused on determining current and required stakeholder commitment levels, and the knowledge base giving rise to these attitudes. Building on this analysis stakeholder management strategies should be developed which focus on achieving the required future commitment levels by influencing the knowledge base. The respective movement in commitment level will therefore be driven by communications between the project team and the key stakeholders. As can be seen from Figure 7.7, gaining stakeholders' commitment to change is often vital to achieving project success. Unfortunately project managers rarely appreciate the scale and complexity of the communication tasks involved in gaining commitment, as shown in Figure 7.9.

Project managers must avoid merely focusing on the preparation and circulation of newsletters and briefing papers (that is, raising awareness). As can be seen from Figure 7.9, they have to follow this up with more direct action if they are to gain widespread commitment to the change proposed by the project. If they do not check the stakeholders' understanding they can find opposers use this raised awareness as a basis to attack the project.

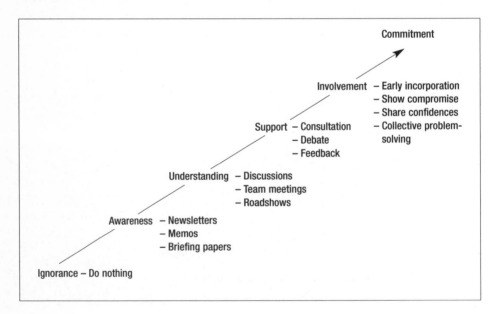

Figure 7.9   Tasks involved in gaining commitment

For ease of reference, the principle features of the various strategies that may need to be adopted have been outlined below in relation to the current knowledge base (Figure 7.8) and commitment levels (Figure 7.7).

Quadrant 1 – Support/Aware

There are three key communication strategies to this group.

Raising commitment   This can generally be achieved by highlighting the role of stakeholders in achieving project success, particularly through ready access to resources and influencing the attitudes of other stakeholders. Prepare for these discussions by developing scenarios showing the effect of, say, late access to resources. Also, if seeking to increase commitment to active support you need to build on the stakeholders' awareness, and their desire to see the project succeed, in preparing them for discussions with other (opposing) stakeholders.

Maintaining commitment   Reinforce their positive view of the project. This is best achieved by repeatedly stressing the alignment between the project and their objectives. Obviously to do this the initial step is to find out what their objectives are.

Lowering commitment   This can be a particularly sensitive situation to deal with. After all these stakeholders want you to succeed, indeed they want to actively help you. So how do you tell them that their active support may actually help the project to fail! A possible way out of this tricky situation is to stress the need for the project team to coordinate the actions of stakeholders in order to ensure maximum benefit for the project. This can then be expanded to include the project team directing the stakeholders' actions. Even where this strategy is well implemented there is always a risk that the stakeholder concerned will see an opportunity to help the project and do, or say, its own thing – with perhaps unforeseen and negative results. This risk can never be fully removed and as such needs constant monitoring.

Quadrant 2 – Support/Ignorant

As noted earlier this support is vulnerable and could easily be lost, even if these stakeholders are initially actively supportive of the project. Support could be lost by opposers raising doubts about whether the project will indeed help these stakeholders achieve their objectives. The project team must discover why these stakeholders are supporting the project. What is in it for them? Remember these stakeholders are ignorant of the details of the project. They are therefore basing their support on assumptions they have made regarding the project. These assumptions need to be checked.

Let's first look at where the stakeholders' assumptions are found to be valid. The project team need to reinforce the stakeholders' support by showing them that the project is indeed what they have assumed. Such confirmation can in itself often result in an increase in the stakeholders' commitment level – from passive to active support.

Now let's look at where the stakeholders' assumptions are not valid. Here we have a potential problem. If active opposers discover this they could use it to change these stakeholders' attitudes. However, this change in attitude could just as easily happen if the project team's communications with the stakeholders merely highlight that the project is not what they thought. So should the project team avoid this problem by trying to keep these stakeholders ignorant? There are two main weaknesses in such a passive strategy:

1. You cannot guarantee that the opposers will not fill the resulting communications void with negative messages.
2. You cannot increase commitment level (for example, from passive to active support) if you don't communicate with the stakeholders (Figure 7.9).

We therefore recommend that a proactive strategy is adopted. This must itself be based on an assumption. That is that once the stakeholders are made aware of the project's details their support will turn to opposition. This opposition must then be quickly addressed through the strategy proposed below for Quadrant 3 – Oppose/Ignorant.

Quadrant 3 – Oppose/Ignorant

As noted earlier, this is a key target area for the project team. If the project team do not take the time and effort to communicate with these stakeholders they will be targeted by the active opposers. This could result in a strengthening of their attitudes (from passive to active opposition). You therefore need to discover why they are opposed and be prepared to negotiate to move them to, as a minimum, passive opposition – they may not like the change but will reluctantly accept it. To achieve acceptance of change it is helpful to understand what influences such acceptance. Figure 7.10 provides an outline of factors which need to be considered and addressed in order to influence someone's acceptance of change:

1. *New benefits* Relative advantage – how much better does the new arrangement appear?
   ● Will the new IS set-up really help?
   ● Will the bypass really save much time?

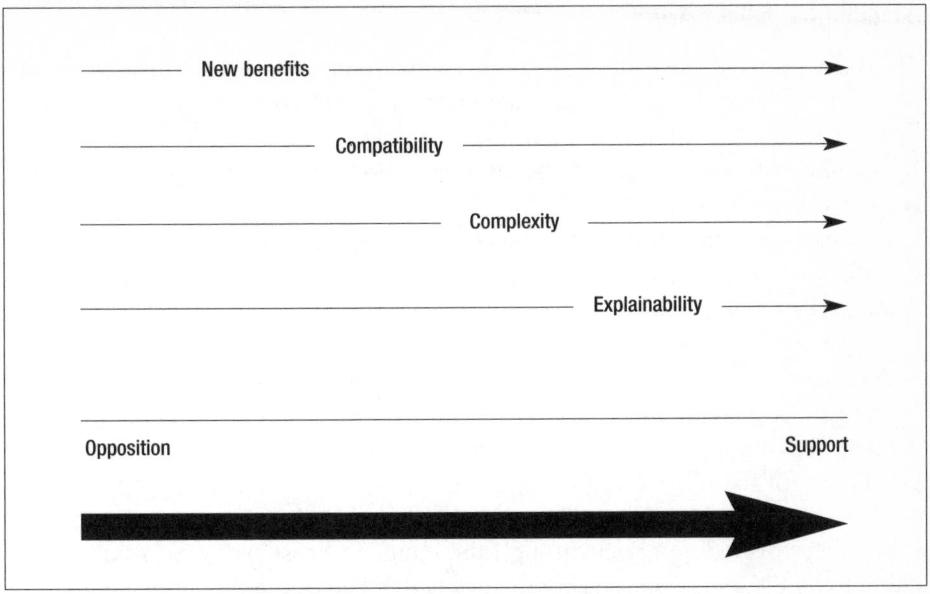

Figure 7.10   What affects the stakeholders' position?

2. *Compatibility*   How much will the stakeholder have to change?
   ● Does the office move mean I'll have to relocate?
3. *Complexity*   How easy is it to adopt the new system?
   ● Can I get it in one go or do I have to go through a dozen different processes?
   ● How many times will you be digging up my road?
4. *Explainability*   How simple is it to explain it all?
   ● Exactly how loud is a decibel?
   ● How smelly is a sewage farm?

Therefore the key elements of this strategy are:

● discovery of what is influencing the stakeholder's view of the project
● discovery of what changes would be required to influence the stakeholder's acceptance of the project
● framing propositions to the stakeholder in respect of the factors outlined above
● negotiating with the stakeholder to achieve acceptance while minimizing the changes required.

Quadrant 4 - Oppose/Aware

This is the most difficult situation to deal with. You are starting with stakeholders who, on the analysis carried out, have knowledge of your project and based on this are opposed to what you are trying to achieve.

Initially the same strategy should be adopted as for Oppose/Ignorant. However, there needs to be recognition that there may be little or no possibility of moving these stakeholders to a position of support for the project. This should not stop you from trying. A visible, positive change in attitude of one of these stakeholders will greatly enhance your chances of increasing or maintaining the commitment levels of other stakeholders.

A note of caution needs to be raised. A lot of energy could be wasted trying to change these stakeholders' attitudes, energy which would probably be better used on stakeholders in one of the other quadrants. Therefore be prepared for the possibility (probability) that these stakeholders will never change their attitude. As they have been identified as key stakeholders they therefore, by our definition, have power over the project through the control of resources. So what are you going to do if these resources are not available? The development of contingency measures to deal with this eventuality has to be a priority task for the project team and is indeed a key feature of the management strategy for these stakeholders.

MONITOR AND REVIEW

The position and level of commitment of various stakeholders with regards to the analysis carried out above will constantly change as their knowledge base about the project changes. Also, new stakeholders may appear. Therefore the various steps shown in Figure 7.3 and outlined above need to be revisited at regular intervals. A question to ask in these regular reviews is 'Are the various stakeholders where you want them to be at this point in time?' Remember that you can't win them all. Focus on gaining the support of those who control key resources and those with the highest influence on project success or failure.

HINTS AND TIPS

Here are some key points in a stakeholder management strategy:

1. Avoid helping to build opposing coalitions.
2. Become known as the monopoly supplier of information.
3. Respond quickly and appropriately to negative impressions.
4. Encourage supporters to meet and reinforce each other.

5. Don't abdicate responsibility for dealing with objectors outside the project team.
6. Use supporters to convert waverers. People are often less suspicious of an intermediary than the company or organization promoting the project.
7. Stress benefits not features.
8. Be prepared to change.
9. Plan ahead.
10. Be sensitive to changes in the business or political environment.

And remember the following:

1. Stakeholders must be identified.
2. Important stakeholders have power *and* an interest.
3. Stakeholder analysis and management is vital for project success.
4. Stakeholders' attitudes change throughout the project life cycle.
5. Dealing with stakeholders is often an intuitive process.

ACKNOWLEDGEMENT

The authors would like to highlight the support and insights provided by Liam Fitzpatrick of CGI Corporate Consulting.

REFERENCE AND FURTHER READING

BS6079 (1996), *Guide to Project Management*, British Standards Institute, London.

8 Managing conflict, persuasion and negotiation

Bob Graham

Managing a project is almost by definition managing conflict, because the success of a project is often measured by the conflicting goals of producing a quality product at a low cost and to a quick deadline. These very goals are in conflict because a quality product often requires a higher cost and a longer deadline. A project can be done faster, but that often requires an increase in budget or a decrease in quality. You can save money on the budget, but that usually results in a decrease in product quality or an increase in project duration. In addition, the project stakeholders are often in conflict. The project represents something new and thus upsets the status quo. The departmental directors who supply the project team members might well want those people working on departmental rather than project work. In fact, the department directors may be fighting each other for headcount and so do not want to send anyone over to a project that may be associated with another department. Thus it seems that project management is conflict management as projects are built on conflicting goals and priorities. Managing all these conflicts often becomes the chief job of the project manager.

Managing this conflict requires the ability to persuade others in the organization to act in ways that will benefit the project. The concept of persuasion and negotiation is used in project management because the project leader typically does not have the command relationship of authority that is present in most departmental organizations. I do not know how many times I have heard statements like 'The problem in this organization is that the project leaders have all of the responsibility, but none of the authority.' To this comment I usually respond 'Welcome to project work'. In the process of project leadership, the lack of direct authority over project team members and other project stakeholders is considered the normal state of affairs. Successful project leaders realize that they must develop their powers of persuasion and negotiation in order to get the project completed.

This chapter will discuss some of the strategies the project manager can use to avoid and resolve conflict. We begin by examining the sources of conflict, for if these sources can be eliminated much potential conflict can be avoided. This is followed by discussion of some techniques for resolving those conflicts that cannot be avoided. Finally, the importance of information in the conflict process is explored.

AVOIDING CONFLICT

UNDERSTANDING SOURCES OF CONFLICT

Prevention of conflict is the first step in managing conflict. It is therefore important first to understand the sources of conflict and work to eliminate those sources so they do not affect the project team. Most conflicts on projects arise from differences about the project goals, the utilization of resources on project teams or are a result of departmental differences or grudges. They arise because a person or a group of people feel frustrated in their ability to achieve their goals. Additional conflict can arise due to interpersonal differences or opposing points of view. The conflict develops out of a basic lack of or unwillingness to understand the other party's position (Pinto 1996). Thus to prevent conflict we begin by examining the sources of conflict, the various people involved in conflict and their points of view.

There are a variety of people in the organization who need to be influenced in favour of the project. One important group is the members of the project team. As these people typically do not report to the project leader, they must be influenced and motivated to devote their best work to the project effort. However, these people come from different departments and may have different work styles and values. In addition, people from one department may have stereotypes of people from other departments and may treat team members as the stereotype rather than the person. Also, it is natural to see one's own departmental aspect as most important for the success of the project, and thus feel that most resources should be allocated to that aspect. For example, people from Production who come to meetings on time may be irritated by people from Marketing who are late. All team members may see those from Accounting as just 'bean counters' to be ignored, and those from Engineering may feel that theirs is the most important aspect of the project and should get most of the resource allocation. The potential for conflict is high.

Another important group of stakeholders is the departmental directors; those people who supply the resources to complete the project. Your project is only one of many projects that they must consider, so they too must be influenced to supply good people for the project. Indeed, conflict can occur in the allocation of people. In addition, departmental directors may be fighting among themselves over organizational priorities, and this will be reflected in your project. An important department is Finance, which supplies the monetary resources for the project. Project managers and team members usually feel that not enough financial resources are allocated, and this is a continuing source of conflict.

The group of senior managers must also be influenced to support this project, as projects are seldom successful without top management support (Pinto and Slevin 1987). Often one or more government agencies must also be included on the stakeholder list. The goals of both these groups could be quite opposed to those of the project team.

Finally, there are the end-users of the project, the people who will benefit most from the project completion, but who often give only lukewarm support as the project progresses. The needs of this group are often hard to pin down and change as the project progresses. The moving target of 'satisfying end-user expectations' often frustrates team members who may be used to more static job specifications. The pool of potential conflict is wide and deep here.

MOTIVATING CONFLICTING PARTIES

The second step in managing conflict is to ensure that all parties to any conflict or potential conflict are motivated to find a solution or prevent the conflict from occurring. This occurs when people see it as being in their best interest to solve or prevent conflict. People can change their opinion and even see another's point of view if they feel it is advantageous to them. People do not usually continue behaving in a way that is detrimental to their achieving their own interests. The same is true for other project stakeholders such as your peers and superiors, as well as functional managers (department directors) who will be supplying the members of your team. The successful project manager will develop an influence strategy for these stakeholder groups as well as for team members to show them that conflict is not in their best interest.

DEVELOPING AN INFLUENCE STRATEGY

The first step in developing an influence strategy is to produce a list of potential stakeholder groups. The next step is to develop a list of key people in these stakeholder groups. For example, within the project team, the core team members are probably the most important. Within the senior management group, the top manager who proposed this project and those that are ultimately supplying the manpower are probably most important. There may also be one customer that is more important than the others.

The next step is to ask yourself why these individuals should support your project. That is, what benefit will they derive from a successful project? If you are unsure of the benefit that key individuals might derive, you might want to discuss it with them. From understanding who benefits from this project you can develop a list of potential allies, along with the knowledge of the benefits you need to deliver to develop and maintain their support. These benefits are an important element in resolving conflict. A valuable complement to the list of 'allies' is a list of 'enemies', that is a list of key individuals who do not initially support the project. Although these people are not really 'enemies', they may not see the benefit of the project or may see it as detrimental to their success or that of the organization. It is important to understand why people do not support the project and then work to overcome their objections as the project progresses. Remember that all enemies are potential allies, if they can see the project as being in their best interest. Chapter 7 gives advice on identifying stakeholders. Figure 7.2 shows a way of viewing enemies and allies:

- those who are in favour of the project and those who are against it
- from these two groups, those who can influence the outcome and those who cannot.

THE REWARD/RISK FACTOR IN MINIMIZING CONFLICT

The key factor in influencing anyone to do anything, including resolving a conflict, is to ensure that the rewards for doing it are greater than the risks involved. The assumption is if people understand and value the rewards for being on your project, and if you have taken the steps to minimize the risks involved in gaining the reward, they will see project work as being in their best interest. This way you can influence them to work on or otherwise support the project and minimize any potential conflict because it will be in their best interest to do so.

Reward – perception of value

Most projects will have value to the organization, as well as value to the individual. The project manager must think clearly through the questions of 'Why are we doing this project?' and 'What are the potential benefits for the people who work on or support this project?' The project manager must then ensure that the potential team members and other stakeholders fully understand the nature of these benefits.

Risk – perception of loss

Most projects will also have potential risks to the organization and potential project participants. The nature of these risks is subjective, and the evaluation of these risks is often a function of the individuals' risk preference profile. To begin to understand these risks, the project manager must ask the question 'What will the organization or the individuals potentially lose if they participate in this project?' Once this list is developed, the project manager must work to ensure that the potential losses are minimized. This information must then be passed on to potential project participants and stakeholders.

Thus the key to developing influence is to maximize the value while minimizing the risks. If the perception of value exceeds the perception of risk, the individuals will be motivated to work on or support the project. If the perception of risk exceeds the perception of value, the individuals will not be so motivated and may work against the completion of the project.

INFLUENCING TEAM MEMBERS

When some managers think of value for team members, they think of money. Many project leaders then lament that they have little control over the salaries of the project team members. However, experience indicates that money is only one part of motivation. Indeed, there are many aspects of projects that people find inherently rewarding and of value. The project leader must use these non-monetary aspects to maximum benefit. Some of these values are discussed below.

Satisfying customer requirements

This is the *raison d'être* of any project. It is also one of the principal benefits to all project stakeholders, and one of the most useful levers to use for managing conflict. Whenever two parties are in conflict over product features it is useful to focus on customer requirements and move away from focusing on which party is 'right'.

Doing something new/learning a new skill

By definition, a project is something new in the organization. People generally enjoy variety in their work, and thus find value in doing something new and different. Most projects involve developing new technology or developing a new application for old technology. Either way the team members often learn some new skill. This aspect enhances people's self-worth, and also their future marketability. Learning and applying the latest methods or technology is rewarding for many people. In addition, learning a new skill often helps people to add value to the organization, enhancing the organizational skill set.

Networking and travel

Most projects cut across departmental lines, and this gives people exposure to other departments. These contacts can increase individuals' organization networks, as well as general knowledge about what they do in other parts of the organization.

Developing a unique product

Most work in organizations involves repetition. Being on a team doing something new and unique can be rewarding. People also find much satisfaction in being able to point to a finished product and say 'I was on the team that made that product.'

Positive visibility with senior management

This is an important reward for many people. In fact this may be one of the most important rewards held by project team members. People often feel it is to their advantage to be viewed positively by upper management. A conflict can often be managed by reminding conflicting parties that their conflict will not look good to upper management and that they should resolve it quickly.

However, there are also many risks associated with something as uncertain as a project.

Negative visibility with senior management

The project leader must remember that there are two sides to the visibility coin. In some organizations, being associated with a failed project is another step closer to the exit door. Thus a good track record helps to recruit project team members. However, if the project leader is new at the job, he or she must display a lot of enthusiasm at the beginning of the project. If the project leader is very enthusiastic about the potential success of the project, potential team members feel there is a higher chance of success (which, of course, helps lead to success, thus becoming a self-fulfilling prophecy). If the project leader is not enthusiastic, then potential team members will feel there is little chance for success and will thus not be motivated to join the project team.

No reward for project work

Lack of reward for project work is a typical problem in organizations that are new to project management. Reward systems and performance appraisals are typically departmentally based, as they should be. This means that organization members typically see their future, promotions, salary and the like tied to their performance in departments. The project leader, however, is attempting to get these people to join project teams, and there will be little motivation to do so unless the work on the project is also appraised and is counted as a part of the performance appraisal and review. The project leader must work to ensure that the project work will be used in performance appraisal and complete said appraisals for all member of the core team.

Out of sight, out of mind

This is an associated risk. Potential team members may feel that if they are not working at all times on department work, then the department managers will 'forget' them and perhaps overlook them if a promotion is available. Thus the project leader must have a system for continually informing departmental managers about the work of their department members.

A more exciting project may come along

There is not much the project leader can do about this fear, except be certain that the potential team members are fully aware of just how exciting this project is going to be.

The project leader must take steps to maximize the perceived benefits and to minimize perceived risk. In addition, team members must be made aware of the potential risks and rewards. This is an important part of the conflict resolution process.

INFLUENCING OTHER STAKEHOLDERS

Numerous studies of successful projects point to the need for top management support, as well as the support of other project stakeholders (Wateridge 1995). Thus a part of the task of project leadership is influencing others to support your project. Influencing upper management and other stakeholders is very similar to influencing team members.

To begin with, the project leader must realize that influencing project stakeholders is a process, not an event. That is, some project leaders will hold stakeholder influencing events, such as a project start-up workshop, and feel that the influence has been set for the project. They often feel that their project will maintain a constant, high priority. However, priorities change, and stakeholders' feelings about and attention to a given project also change over time. So while a project start-up workshop is an excellent event for gaining support for a project, it is to be seen as only one event in a long and continuous process of developing and maintaining project support.

The process of developing project support begins by identifying the major project stakeholders, as was done above. For the next step the project leader must determine what value these various groups will obtain from a successful project. And for those that are not initially supportive of the project, what loss they feel the project will bring them. Common values received from projects are shown for the stakeholder groups as follows.

Senior management

The common value for upper management is that the project will help to support a corporate strategy, such as entering a new market. If the strategy is successful, then the project will ultimately help to lead to higher profitability and other corporate goals. It is important that the project leader realizes just what strategy it is that the project is supporting. As projects unfold they are often scrutinized as to their expense, and are often felt to be expendable at budget review time. It is important that the project leader reminds upper management what strategy will suffer if the project does not receive continued support.

Customers/end-users

The customers and end-users are the people who will gain benefit from the use of the end product. To satisfy the customers the project leader must be continually in touch with what the customers want from the product, as well as what they really expect from it. Experienced project leaders understand that what customers say they want, and what they really expect, are often two very different things. It is thus a task of the project leader continually to probe to discover what it is that the customers and end-users really expect from the end product.

There are two parts to discovering customer expectations. One is to develop a mindset of continuous exploration. This means the project team expects and welcomes a sequence of constant changes and suggestions from the customers and end-users. In the past, these changes were seen as irritants that delayed project progress. Now they should be seen as additional information that helps to ensure project success. The second part is using a series of prototypes to evoke responses. It is a fact of life that most people cannot really tell you what they expect from a product until they have experience of it. Developing prototypes allows customers to have this experience and to ask the classic question 'Well, how come it doesn't do this or that?' Of course, the customer never asked for it to do this or that, but the experience of the prototype will uncover that it expected it to do this or that. Obtaining customer reaction early and often can eliminate potential conflict at the end of a project.

Department directors

This is the group of stakeholders that will be supplying the people to complete the project work. It is assumed that all of the people working on a project will be 'on loan' from various departments in the organization. It is thus important that the project leader consider the needs and desires of the managers of those departments.

Department managers are also trying to implement corporate strategy, so a knowledge of how the project supports corporate strategy is also important to gaining their support. However, department managers are also occupied with the more immediate task of scheduling people to perform the tasks of the department, as well as supporting other projects. Thus the more immediate questions run along the lines of 'What people do you want, for how much of their time, and when will they be finished?' It is thus important that the project leader reviews project plans, schedules and progress with department managers on a regular basis. The more complete and accurate information they have from you, the better they will be able to schedule people to meet the other demands that are placed on their departments. This will help to develop and maintain their support for your project.

Other stakeholders

There may be some groups or individuals, even among those mentioned above, who will not initially support the project. With these people it is important that the project leader determines what they have at risk or what they feel they have to lose from successful completion of the project. Many times this feeling of risk and/or loss is due to misinformation or false assumptions about the project. Thus to gain the support of these groups or individuals, the project leader must discover what their assumptions are and work to inform. In fact, the project leader must do more than inform, as talk is cheap. He or she must demonstrate that the results of the project will not result in the loss the others expect. This is a long process and it often takes place over the life of the project. But it has many rewards.

For example, when I became a project manager it was at a college that did not have a computer when I walked in the door. Part of my job was to computerize the registration, billing and housing function. At that time it was assumed by most employees that when things went onto the computer everyone would lose their jobs. Gaining cooperation was difficult as everyone treated me like the grim reaper. I seemed to be in conflict with everyone until I understood the source of their perception of risk. When I was able to convince them they would not lose their jobs, and also demonstrated the value of the computer, much of the conflict evaporated.

RESOLVING CONFLICT

Despite our best efforts, conflict happens and must be resolved. Pinto (1996) suggests three methods of resolving conflict which he classifies as confrontation, diffusion and avoidance.

Confrontation

Confrontation methods seek the sources of the conflict so that conflicting parties can discuss the sources and work to resolve the conflict. A typical technique is a problem-solving meeting where the conflicting parties and the project manager meet and discuss conflict causes and possible resolution. This is a long process, frequently accompanied by high emotions from the parties concerned. If the meeting is not handled well, it can solidify conflict and ill-will, making possible resolution much more difficult. As many project managers do not have the skill or the time to do this, obtaining outside help is recommended for this method.

Diffusion

Diffusion methods try to diffuse the conflict for enough time for conflicting parties to work it out. One diffusion technique is to appeal to the common goal of the project, emphasizing that 'we are all in this together'. Another is compromise, the classic 'give and take' in which parties cease conflict because they get something they want while they give something the other party wants. While diffusion techniques address the conflict directly they do not require the discovery of the root causes of that conflict.

Avoidance

Avoidance methods avoid directly addressing the conflict source while seeking to resolve it. One technique is for the project manager to send signals that the conflict is not a good idea. This is an attempt to show people it is not in their best interest to continue the conflict. Another technique is forced separation, that is hopefuly the conflict will go away if the parties are physically separated. However, this is not good for project management, which relies on close interaction of team members. A third technique is forced togetherness where the project manager gives two conflicting parties a task where they must work harmoniously together to be successful. In this way both parties see conflict resolution as being in their best interest.

AN EXAMPLE OF FORCED TOGETHERNESS

In a large telephone company there were two groups, among others, who were responsible for installation of PBX switches for corporations. Two particular groups were in conflict and had been in conflict for quite some time. One group had a marketing orientation; the other was made up of old line telephone engineers. The first group was responsible for determining customer requirements. The second group was responsible for designing and installing the equipment to solve the customer problems. This meant that the second group got its instructions from the first group. The marketing function, and many of the members of that group, was new to the corporation. The engineering function and most of the engineers had been a part of the company since the dawn of time. Both departments were very suspicious of each other and had various derogatory terms to describe one another. They did not like to work together.

A recent switch installation had gone badly. The telephone users claimed the switch did not meet their needs. They were furious and threatened to change companies for the next switch. Senior management of the telephone company demanded that this important customer be satisfied with the next installation. Marketing blamed Engineering for not correctly designing a switch that met customer needs, while Engineering blamed Marketing for not correctly determining user requirements. Both sides pointed to the other and said, 'We would not have this problem if those guys would just do their job correctly!' Obviously the level of conflict was getting in the way of understanding the true source of user dissatisfaction.

A project team with members from both departments was formed for the next switch installation. We began conflict management with departmental managers, convincing them that since senior management was interested in this customer, it was in their best interest to help resolve this conflict. As above so below. We also convinced all team members it was in their best interest to work together. At project team meetings we focused on understanding the end-user requirements. We initiated a process of forced interaction where two team members from each department went together to interview users, so they could understand together

129

what the requirements were. While doing this they discovered the source of the problem was simple communications errors. By focusing on eliminating these errors and truly understanding customer and end user requirements, the conflict was resolved for that project.

THE POWER AND VALUE OF INFORMATION

One of the final sources of conflict is lack of reliable information. Project leaders need to see themselves as the ultimate disseminators of information. Because of the uncertainty that surrounds most projects, they tend to generate much anxiety among the stakeholders and this can be a potential source of conflict. This anxiety is usually concerning the outcome, cost, final schedule and resource requirements of the project. Information is the only tool that the project leader has to relieve this anxiety. The project leader will find that he or she can have a large influence on the members of the organization by providing timely and complete information regarding the salient aspects of the project.

The first step in developing a project management information system is to determine what information it is that the stakeholders need to help them achieve their objectives. Some texts would advise the project leader to begin with a list of stakeholders and proceed to ask each of them what information they need about the project. However, experience has shown that the response to such a question does not reveal all that is needed. Many people find it difficult to answer a question about what data they need. They will give you an answer, but when the data is presented, they typically answer that it is not what they wanted. This often leaves the project leader puzzled and frustrated. The fact is that most people do not think in terms of data, but rather in terms of questions. Therefore, instead of asking 'What data do you need?' it is better to ask 'What questions do you have about this project?' Then the project leader and the stakeholder can work together to develop a set of information that answers those questions. Good information is that which answers stakeholders' questions, is easy for them to understand and is there when they need it. This requires that the project leader understands the questions and associated information from the stakeholders' points of view. The project management information system should then be developed to satisfy their needs, in much the same way that the entire project is developed to satisfy the needs of the customer/end-users.

QUESTIONS ON OUTCOME

The questions about outcome are normally of three types.

Functionality

The first is about what the final product will do when it is completed. This is a question for the project leader as well as the project stakeholders as the specifications will be changing as the project proceeds. The project leader must guard against the problem of suggesting a certain function will be available before it is certain that it will indeed be in the final product. So answers to questions about outcome should be in two parts. The first contains features that have definitely been decided. The second contains a list of features that are being considered. This list should be updated regularly and be distributed automatically to all stakeholders.

Success

The second question about outcome is the 'Will it be successful?' type. Stakeholders want to know how this product compares with the competition, and its probability of market acceptance. The best way to answer these questions is to summarize the information gleaned from the customer or end-user representatives, show how the product is being designed to address those expectations and pass this to the stakeholders. If this cannot be done for competitive reasons (secrecy), then the stakeholders should be assured that it is indeed taking place.

Market

A third outcome question is of the 'market segment' type. Stakeholders often want to know what market the product is aimed to satisfy. Thus the project leader needs to be continually aware of and searching for potential applications and markets for the product, and passing this information on to the stakeholders.

QUESTIONS ABOUT THE SCHEDULE

Of course, the classic schedule question is 'When will it be ready?' Associated questions concern availability of prototypes and milestone reviews. This means that an updated schedule should be always available to stakeholders to answer these questions.

QUESTIONS ABOUT RESOURCE REQUIREMENTS

Projects have a way of using up countless hours of resources, much of which is usually said to be unexpected. This often frustrates the department directors who are supplying that resource and is a continuing source of conflict. Their questions normally revolve around how much of the resource you are going to need, and when the resource will be again available to the department. Project leaders are understandably hesitant to answer such questions, as projections for requirements are difficult to make when you are doing something for the first time. In addition, initial estimates have a quality of being 'cast in stone', so that future changes in requirements cause friction with the department directors. Thus the requirements should be presented with a 'here is what we know so far' quality. The project leader should not just produce estimates and send them to the department directors. Rather he or she should personally explain all of the assumptions that contributed to that estimate, and indicate all of the factors that could cause that estimate to change.

Department directors, as are all of us, are much more amenable to change if they understand the reason for the change. It is up to the project leader to ensure that they know the reasons for all changes. Often just knowing the reasons for a change can eliminate a potential conflict. In addition to providing information that answers their questions, good information should also be there when it is most needed. Having the information available to stakeholders is often not enough. The project leader should attempt to determine when it is that the information will most likely be needed. Some simple questions to stakeholders like 'When do you usually discuss this project?' or 'What meetings do you go to where questions about this project come up?' can often reveal the best time to provide the information. For example, if there is a regular meeting where the project is discussed, it would be good to provide the information the day before that meeting. In that way the stakeholder could arrive at the meeting with the latest information. Timely information is current information that arrives just before the person needs it.

As a final note, it is important to remember that timely, accurate information is useless unless the person who is using the information understands what is being presented. Many people are not comfortable with information presented on Gantt charts and network diagrams. Thus the first few times that information is supplied, the project leader may need to personally review the format with the stakeholders to ensure that they fully understand what they are being presented with. If they cannot work with network diagrams and the like, then a different format should be developed with which they are comfortable.

Always remember that the information is being produced to relieve anxiety and avoid or resolve conflict. If the people cannot understand the information, it will actually increase the very anxiety it was designed to reduce. So the information should conform to the person, rather than expecting the person to conform to the information. In summary, good information answers their questions, is there when they need it and is easy to understand.

CONCLUSIONS

It has been shown in this chapter that the task of running a successful project requires conflict avoidance and resolution. This requires leading by influence rather than authority. The keys to developing this influence lie in understanding individuals' risk/reward relationship, as well as the power of information. It was argued that the project leader can manage conflict and influence individuals to do their best on a project if team members perceive that it is in their best interest, and that the benefits outweigh the risks. The project leader must use information to show people the potential rewards, as well as the way risks are being addressed.

Developing influence is a process, not an event. In everyday terms, this means that the project leader can never really order team members to complete a task, but must persuade them, over and over again. The approach is for the project leader to ask him- or herself 'What is the benefit in doing this task?' and then approach the team members by first stressing the benefit. The project leader should then listen carefully to their responses, as their perceived risks are often contained in these responses. If the project leader can give information that shows how he or she is addressing those perceived risks, while continuing to show benefit, then the project leader will be leading by influence.

Such influence is normally much more effective than authority. However, it takes more time. The project leader will often feel the urge to just say 'Do it' in order to get things done. This may often be seen as a short-run necessity, but it leads to a long-run disaster. Use it sparingly.

REFERENCES AND FURTHER READING

Pinto, J. K. (1996), *Power & Politics in Project Management*, Project Management Institute, Sylva, NC.

Pinto, J. K. and Slevin, D. P. (1987), 'Critical success factors in effective project implementation', in D. I. Cleland and W. R. King (eds), *Project Management Handbook*, 2nd edition, Van Nostrand Reinhold, New York.

Wateridge, J. F. (1995), 'IT projects: a basis for success', *International Journal of Project Management*, **13**(3).

9 Managing culture

David Rees

You are looking forward to a new project challenge as you wave goodbye to Johnny and the kids at London Heathrow. You've done well these past few years, moving through the hierarchy of a large UK multinational telecommunications corporation to your present job of International Project Manager. Certainly your career path has taken a number of twists and turns since those days 15 years ago when you started out as a young graduate electronics engineer in what was then a public sector monopoly. How things have changed during that time. Moving through the ranks of technical specialist to supervisor, middle manager and now, since privatization, to the world of project management – and a senior one at that! And still only 37 years old, one of a handful of women in a work environment dominated by men. The organization itself has been through dramatic transformation:

- from non-profit-making public ownership to a commercial enterprise driven by a doctrine of maximizing shareholder value
- from over 300,000 employees to just half that number now
- from a mechanistic bureaucracy to a fleet-footed matrix structure.

You're rewarded on achievement – not just for turning up to work each day. On top of this, the business now operates across national boundaries. Global customers have to be served (and delighted), strategic alliances managed and international joint ventures pursued. Yes, Bangkok beckons. But this is a journey that has put a number of questions in your mind – the answers to which cannot exclusively be found in your company training room. You've been briefed by experts, both technical and behavioural, but you know that Project Poppit will be different from anything you've experienced before. Well, that's the nature of projects!

Reflecting upon this situation we can identify a number of elements that will be important determinants of project success. The focus of our interest for this chapter is the cultural factors. It may be useful at this point to consider what we mean by 'culture'.

DEFINITIONS OF CULTURE

A starting point is to go back to the original meaning of the word *kultura* as the ancient Greeks interpreted it meaning 'to act upon nature'. Or the Latin form *cultura* – 'cultivating or tilling (the land)'. The general concept here is one of status and growth and can be applied in both a physical sense (agriculture) and a development mode (enlightenment, refinement).

Some interesting definitions of culture have been offered by two key researchers in this field:

> Culture is the collective programming of the mind, which distinguishes the member of one group or society from those of another.
>
> (Hofstede 1994)

> A fish only discovers its need for water when it is no longer in it. Our own culture is like water to a fish. It sustains us. We live and breathe through it.
>
> (Trompenaars 1993)

Further, there are varying contexts in which the term and its derivatives are used. We talk of personal tastes, manners and social etiquette as being 'culture-related'. Groups whose focus is on intellectual and artistic activities are often classified as 'cults'. Organizations and their subsets may take on identifiable 'corporate cultures'. A project management culture is an example of such a subset.

As Paula sets off for Thailand we can think of a range of culture-bound factors that may affect her success as a project manager:

- her own status in terms of technical qualifications, age and gender
- the organizational climate and management style under which she will operate
- the whole concept of project management as a business philosophy
- the local and cross-border environments in which she works.

Additionally, in her role she will have to manage a number of cultural issues related to the project stakeholders:

1. Does the customer understand the approach to service delivery?
2. Do project team members view time management in the same way?
3. Is project planning seen as a valuable tool for effective performance?

CULTURE IN BUSINESS

Why should we be interested in business culture? To understand 'business culture' we need to consider three segments of what Garrison (1998) has referred to as the 'cultural iceberg'. A brief background to this conceptualization will make the 'iceberg' model (Figure 9.1) meaningful. Since 'culture' has been earmarked as a discipline of study in its own right we have seen many branches of the social sciences stake their claim for leading the theoretical development of the subject.

1. Anthropologists have been interested in the physiological development of the human species and the associated rituals, myths and beliefs that parallel these growth stages.
2. Sociologists tend to focus on the study of man as a social creature in their attempts to explain how communities and societies evolve.

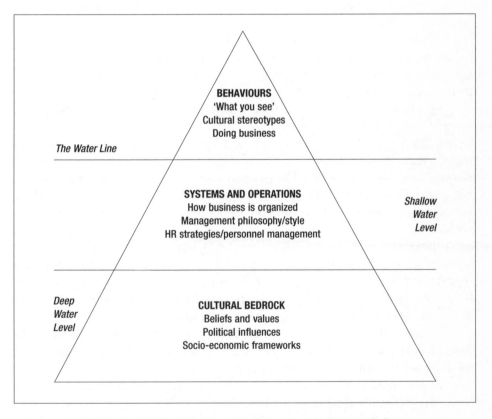

Figure 9.1   The iceberg model of inter-cultural business analysis
Source: Adapted from Garrison T. (1998), *International Culture*, 2nd edition, Elm Publications, Huntingdon

3. Psychologists concentrate on mental processes and behaviours within the individual and their impact on others.
4. Political scientists examine power, authority and control structures within geographic, territorial and societal boundaries.
5. Economists attempt to understand the systems of exchange that enable resources to be developed and utilized in a range of human groupings.

Two conclusions can be drawn from the studies that emerge from these differing disciplines. First, these approaches help us to understand human behaviour and, in particular, management behaviour. Second, the understanding of culture gained from these disciplines can impact upon the performance of business organizations – including the management of projects. The implications of such conclusions are profound. Business success becomes a function of the degree to which we understand the effects of human behaviour and are able to act on such knowledge. This is the reason why organizations are keen to improve their management of business culture – they see this as an opportunity to gain competitive advantage.

Until quite recently an interlocking model bringing together these disciplines to help us understand business culture had been missing. The 'cultural iceberg' helps to rectify this and, in turn, provides an opportunity to manage our business methodologies, such as project management, more effectively (Figure 9.1). If we imagine the iceberg at sea we can only physically see about 10 per cent of its mass. We are not immediately aware of what supports and shapes it beneath the waves. The 'iceberg' tip is a straightforward way of depicting the 'touchables' of a society. What we do not see are the 'untouchable' (or hidden) elements. Yet these elements are the very building blocks upon which our societies and organizations are based. They provide the superstructure and cultural 'fabric' from which behaviours will surface. The base of the iceberg represents the cultural 'bedrock' upon which the superstructure is constructed.

Trompenaars and Hampden-Turner (1997) likened culture to layers of an onion, each layer revealing another layer until the core is reached. The core represents *implicit culture* which are the basic assumptions on which a society is built. The middle layers suggest the underlying norms and values that have grown out of the core while the outer layers depict visible manifestations or *explicit culture* (Figure 9.2). Other writers have used the analogy of the lily being drawn from its structure beneath the surface of the pond – we see the flower but we don't see the substantive mass which gives it life. Similarly we can think of a tree with its roots in the ground as the 'bedrock', the trunk and branches as the 'superstructure' and the leaves, buds or flowers as the tangible outcomes of its existence.

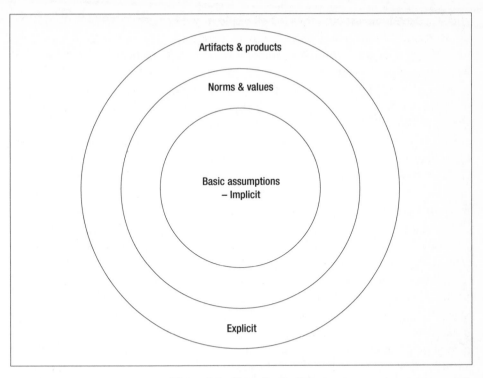

Figure 9.2　The cultural onion

Source: Trompenaars and Hampden-Turner (1997), *Riding the Waves of Culture*, published by Nicholas Brealey Publishing, London

Let us take another look at the iceberg model to help us acquire a better understanding of how business culture develops.

At its base we have the cultural bedrock, foundations of the culture that are reflected in the evolution of the political and economic systems that pertain to that cultural environment. Garrison calls these *policonomy* factors. The way in which these systems themselves have evolved are sometimes extremely hard to trace. Often the very source of the bedrock has disappeared. Liken this to the discovery of the source of the River Nile – very difficult to find! To penetrate the policonomy of a particular societal culture we may need to go back a long way in history to discover the storyline. Some of it gets lost in the mists of time. Sometimes we arrive at a stage of investigation where seeking further evidence or proof becomes pointless – we are trapped in time. What becomes more important and relevant is how we can then work forward to the present day culture that we wish to understand better. Historical policonomy gives us some great clues. Social frameworks are created reflecting the key value and belief sets born out of the bedrock. These form the superstructure features from which our management

139

and work systems emerge. So, for example, if we have a society which is based upon unquestioning obedience to rulers endowed with 'divine rights', we can expect rigid structures of management control and a management culture which will not tolerate dissent.

At the top of the iceberg we are at the behavioural 'output' level. This is our experiential level where we physically and mentally interact with cultural artefacts. We touch, taste, feel, smell and see culture. Our intuitive sense – the 'sixth' sense – could be likened to raising the state of 'cultural subconsciousness' to a level of consciousness – emotions, attitudes and beliefs that are there but can't always be rationalized. We move from the systems level of culture to the individual level – the personal experience. And this is where managers really feel the impact of culture on their day-to-day activities.

Managers are, of course, in a unique pivotal position. They themselves are products of the cultural bedrock and the resulting organizational systems. In turn, their task is to manage operations within the prevailing cultural norms of the enterprise. In other words they have a responsibility to administer the activities of the company according to prescribed sets of rules, regulations, processes, procedures and systems. But they also have an opportunity to influence and implement change depending on a variety of factors including their ability to challenge the prevailing corporate culture. This brings us to the heart of our topic – the management of cultures and the particular challenges for project managers. As a summary so far we can see that this methodology of analysing cultures can be applied to varying levels and situations – societal, industrial, corporate, cross-cultural and so forth.

IMPACT OF CULTURE ON PERFORMANCE

Is there any evidence that the management of culture in business can improve organizational performance? The answer is an unqualified 'yes'. Writers and management theorists have been hinting for decades at correlations between organizational culture and performance. Precise measurement of the impact of culture on company and project success will always be difficult. Most of us sense that there must be a strong link but it is difficult to establish the culture/performance tie-up. However, recent research efforts have started to produce more tangible data that builds an increasingly coherent picture of cultural impact on business.

Of outstanding note has been a study published by the Institute of Personnel and Development (IPD 1998). Researchers from Sheffield University and the London School of Economics were keen to determine whether organizational culture significantly predicts variation between companies in their performance and, if so, which aspects of culture appear most important. They interpreted organizational culture as 'the aggregate of employees' perceptions of aspects of the organisation' and developed an Organizational Culture Indicator which identified the cultural dimensions most frequently evaluated in organizations. The results of their investigations enabled them to explain that 29 per cent of the variation in productivity of the companies studied could be attributed to human relations dimensions, confirming their hypothesis in terms of the importance of culture in relation to company performance.

Now let us see how cultural factors impact on project performance.

MANAGING CULTURE IN PROJECTS

Some writers are keen to emphasize that project management is a relatively new, American-initiated approach to achieving business success. It is true that many specific techniques used in managing projects today have been borne out of recent western management experience. These are, of course, discussed in detail elsewhere in this publication.

However, it is well to remember that the construction of the Egyptian Pyramids, the building of the Great Wall of China and the Roman Invasion of Britain were all fine examples of successful large-scale projects. If these projects were being run today, would performance be any better as a result of using contemporary project management techniques? (Forget technological advancements for the moment.) The answer to this is debatable and reminds us of the historical perspectives alluded to above. We should be careful in assuming that technique alone is responsible for 'better' project management. Once again, 'culture' stakes its claim. Consider those examples again. Would a project kick-off meeting with key stakeholders fit the highly autocratic style of the Pharaoh? Would Gantt charts be helpful in Chinese society where time may not be seen as a simple linear progression? And would PERT (program evaluation and review technique) appeal to Caesar's military leadership?

In fact, we do not have to dwell in the depths of history to identify the impact of culture on projects. Project management itself is a culture-bound concept. Some businesses embrace projects as 'a way of doing things' because it sits comfortably with the values and norms of the organization. This approach 'to getting things done' suits one industry better than another. Or maybe the principles of project management are more readily assimilated in a particular society. This discussion is not intended to question the wisdom of managing through a project approach but rather to remind ourselves again that one of the

141

key challenges for project managers is to manage the cultural environment in which the activities are conducted.

In our quest to manage culture effectively let us remind ourselves of the nature of projects. Handy (1985) would describe project-oriented businesses (such as matrix organizations) as forms of a task culture. Projects are originated to achieve specific goals and tend to be objectives-driven. The culture brings together appropriate resources and enables the project manager and the team to deliver as best they know how. The key deliverables are usually measured against specific objectives pertaining to time, cost and quality – the classic project management performance triangle. Handy argues that influence is based more on expert power than on position or personal power. The view on expert power needs to be reconsidered. Plenty of large projects have been managed by non-experts. An example of this is the development of British Airways' Waterside Headquarters at London's Heathrow Airport where human resource specialists were involved as project managers.

Task cultures also breed team cultures which work powerfully to overcome divergent and disparate individual preferences. These draw upon group dynamics to get things done. Consequently, this culture can take on highly adaptable and flexible characteristics. Project teams can be formed at short notice, terminated rapidly and reformed. Individuals can be dedicated members of one team or hold membership of several project groups, each project having potentially different objectives, scale and technical content. Further, team members may play different roles in different project teams. An outstanding example of this form of total project culture is Oticon, the Danish hearing aid company that underwent a radical business transformation during the early 1990s (Morsing 1998). After the enterprise experienced severe difficulties in the 1980s which threatened its very survival, Oticon's new President, Lars Kolind, unveiled a vision, a strategy and a plan to provide the company with strong long-term competitive advantage. His whole approach was driven by establishing a project management culture. The strategic change required was formulated as a business transformation programme consisting of a number of interrelated projects all held together by a unifying vision. The vision was to transform the company from a technology-based culture to a market-focused culture and to change ways of working to achieve the desired goals.

The strategy to manage the cultural change required was to use project management approaches. The whole change programme became known as 'Project 330' with the overall aim of becoming 30 per cent more efficient within three years. Perhaps the most innovative change at Oticon involved a new organizational form and structure. Out went the old hierarchical management system where people were organized into specific functions and in came a new 'spaghetti' way of organizing. The 'spaghetti organization' embraced novel methods of working including multi-tasking, multidisciplinary project teams and self-management. Figure 9.3 captures some of these essential features. In this teamworking model individuals may play a 'normal' role according to their profession and training, but also switch into other roles in different teams. This represents a highly fluid and flexible work environment which can deliver competitive advantage.

Oticon has become a classic case study in how to manage culture. Imagine for a moment how dramatic the effect of transformation was for employees and managers working in the old culture. Suddenly, a revolution in the workplace was taking place. Kolind became the 'project manager as change agent' – big-time! First he created an overarching vision of what the organization needed to achieve and how this could be done. Next he set about project planning – creating objectives, identifying resources and developing a team. Then came implementation – ensuring that the old culture was honoured, bridges burned and the new culture welcomed in.

One lesson to be learned from this experience is how important symbolism can be. Kolind recognized this and ensured that the new culture was consolidated – closing elevators to encourage the use of stairs; refreshment points with flip charts; glass tubes through the building taking away waste paper. These examples remind us not only that culture has to be managed within projects but also that projects themselves often influence cultural change in organizations.

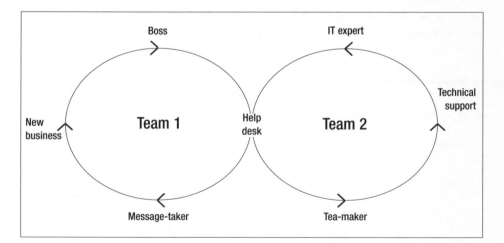

Figure 9.3 Role fluency
© Cultural Fluency Training and Development Ltd 1999

143

MANAGING CULTURAL INTEGRATION

STRATEGIC LEVEL

Events such as mergers, takeovers and acquisitions have become the subject of much attention from business analysts, corporate financiers and company lawyers in their search for competitive advantage. This has placed the 'hard' elements of the enterprise as the priority considerations when doing deals of this type. Far less attention has been paid to the cultural aspects of the deal. Similarly, organizations have experienced serious problems when forming new business entities such as joint ventures, strategic alliances and partnerships. The business strategy seems logical, the numbers work out and the technological advantages are clear. But when it comes to achieving the right 'cultural fit' a disappointing picture emerges (Figure 9.4). A quick tour of some recent research bears this out.

In their book *Smart Alliances*, Harbison and Pekar (1998) have identified cultural differences as one of the key implementation issues that needs to be carefully evaluated and managed during alliance formation. Successful alliance builders, they say, have knowledge of a potential partner's management culture prior to a deal. There is a growing list of alliances where performance has ranged from total failure to non-fulfilment of potential as a result of not achieving effective cultural integration between the alliance members.

Clearly there is a need to conduct due diligence in such situations across a broader range of factors – including cultural factors. So, as a first step to managing the cultural issues of organizational integration, 'cultural due diligence' is a process worth considering. For large deals, business transformation programmes and alliance formation, cultural due diligence should be thought of as a prerequisite before decision-making.

Date	Institution/report	Finding
1987	London Business School	Highlighted lack of personnel and management audit, pre-acquisition, as a key weakness
	People in Business survey	Deals too focused on financial issues
		M&A led by corporate financiers; other professions are needed in M&A teams
1995	Imperial College	Euro cross-border deals found that differences in management style bore a strong correlation to chance of failure
1996	Economist Intelligence Unit	Confirmation of above

Figure 9.4   International mergers, acquisitions and alliances: the failure factor
© Cultural Fluency Training and Development Ltd 2000

Cultural due diligence is a new concept and there are various approaches to conducting the activity involving the measurement of the elements of corporate culture. Many instruments are available to conduct such assessments. Various behavioural aspects can be probed creating profiles of individuals, teams and organizations. Essentially this becomes an audit process where data are collected and analysed, 'culture gaps' identified and a 'culture profile' is drawn up. Figure 9.5 shows such an audit process. Garrison's (1998) Triangle Test is a highly useful audit and diagnostic tool that can be used in a variety of strategic situations: alliance/partnership/joint venture formation; mergers and acquisitions; strategic projects. The test investigates the three cultural segments of the iceberg – behaviours, work systems and bedrock – and can reveal useful profiles of, for example, potential international partners prior to a deal. The scores that can be obtained are depicted in Figure 9.6. The questions contained in the test have inevitably to do with the extent to which business cultures follow a range of patterns from:

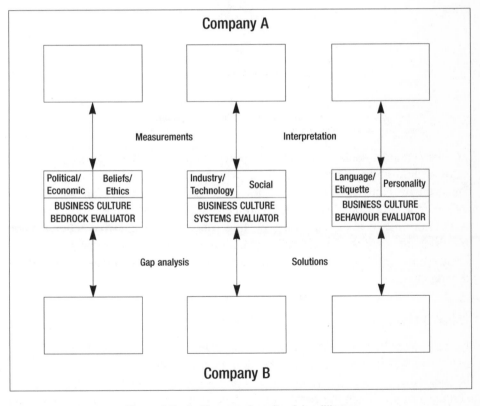

Figure 9.5   Audit process for cultural due diligence
© Cultural Fluency Training and Development Ltd 1999

- individualistic to corporatist bedrock
- materialistic to communitarian work systems
- open to closed behaviours.

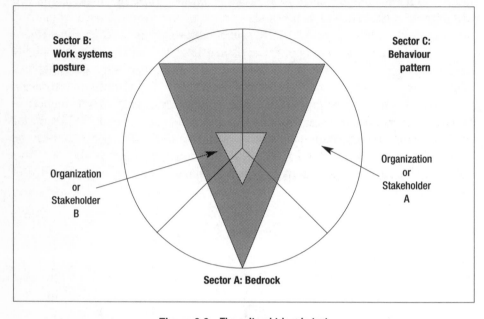

Figure 9.6   The cultural triangle test
Source: Garrison T. (1998), *International Culture*, 2nd edition, Elm Publications, Huntingdon

Results can alert senior executives to potential difficulties arising from national cultural differences. They can indicate whether the project will be significantly impaired by cultural differences and in extreme cases they can significantly influence whether the deal should be done at all. In all cases the test can provide useful information about cultural gaps, how wide they are and what action may be required for a smooth integration plan. Integration planning can be seen as bringing two cultures together as the example of global alliances in Figure 9.7 demonstrates.

PROJECT LEVEL

It can be seen that cultural audit and measurement can be applied to stakeholder management with projects. A list of stakeholders is compiled and a weighting can be applied based on the project manager's expertise and knowledge or other suitable criteria. Then the results of the measurement process can be tabled and a map constructed. This provides the project manager with valuable information

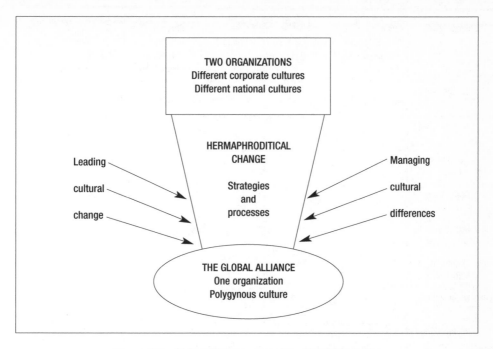

Figure 9.7   Global alliances: managing cultural integration
© Cultural Fluency Training and Development Ltd 1999

which can help him or her manage the cultural aspects of each stakeholder (Figure 9.8). Trompenaars and Hampden-Turner (1997) use the concept of culture mapping to illustrate dilemmas between cultural dimensions at an international level but the 'mapping' idea can be used to plot positions on a range of cultural issues in a mono-domestic environment, such as projects. Another example of culture mapping was provided by John Mole (1995) with the Mole Map, plotting cultural attitudes towards leadership and organization. His map produces a configuration of organic/systematic organizational structures and group/individual leadership styles.

MANAGING INTERNATIONAL CULTURES

It is appropriate at this point to explore the particular challenges of the international project environment. A favoured approach by many researchers in the field of cross-cultural understanding is to establish 'cultural dimensions' (as mentioned earlier) to contrast different attitudes, values and behaviours. Although most writers would suggest a heavy note of caution against cultural

Stakeholder	Type of relationship (strategic/ tactical)	Scale of importance (1–10)	Countries/ cultures	Cultural dimension A (for example cooperation)	Cultural dimension B (for example risk aversion)	And so on
Customers						
Shareholders						
Trade unions						
Community						
Political authorities						
Financial institutions						
Suppliers						
Partners/joint ventures						
Parent/ subsidiary						
Associate						

Figure 9.8   Stakeholder mapping for projects
© Cultural Fluency Training and Development Ltd 1999

stereotyping, the dimensions approach to cultural analysis does offer a pragmatic way of unpicking the cultural onion. Hofstede (1994) and Trompenaars (1993) have produced credible research and provided us with a reliable grouping of dimensions. These are indicated in Figure 9.9.

Using the cultural dimensions developed through Hofstede's famous research on national cultures, Turner (1999) has consolidated fieldwork undertaken by Jessen and arrived at a 'fitness for project management' country ranking table. The scores captured attitudes throughout the project life cycle towards initiation, planning, execution and termination. The country ranking is given in Figure 9.10. The results confirm that project management sits most comfortably as a management philosophy in western cultures. This type of information prior to project start-up can be helpful in managing behaviours across national cultures.

For example, at an operational level conflict will have to be managed at various

Dimension	Refers to
Power distance	Autocracy v. democracy, distribution of influence
Individualism v. collectivism	Focus on individual or group
Universalist v. particularist	Principles of right and wrong; personal relationships
Specific v. diffuse	Legal processes and personal trust
Neutral v. emotional	Objective interactions v. emotional expressions
Uncertainty avoidance	Attitude to risk, uncertainty, ambiguity
Short term v. long term	Perspective on investment returns and results
Achievement v. ascription	Status, performance
Attitudes to time	Emphasis on past, present or future
Internal v. external	Motivation for self or outside world

Figure 9.9 **The Hofstede and Trompenaars cultural dimensions**
Source: Hofstede (1994) and Trompenaars (1993)

1	Germany	10	Sweden
2	Italy	11	Denmark
3	France	12	Japan
4	USA	13	Thailand
5	Netherlands	14	West Africa
6	Norway	15	Philippines
7	Great Britain	16	Yugoslavia
8	Arab countries	17	Malaysia
9	East Africa		

Figure 9.10 **Country ranking for project management**
Source: Turner (1999)

points during the project. Thomas, Killman and Swierczek (Swierczek 1994) have developed models of conflict-handling styles which can provide insights into differing national styles. Various studies have shown significant contrasts in conflict management on projects, particularly between managers from western cultures and those from the east. In one such study Law (1998) has overlaid the Hofstede dimensions against the Thomas/Killman/Swierczek model enabling us to see once again how culture impacts on key project behaviours such as conflict handling (Figure 9.11).

MULTICULTURAL PROJECT MANAGEMENT

It has become apparent that project managers will need to manage projects differently according to the degree of multiculturism within the project. The key issue here is the manager's choice of performance measures for the project. The

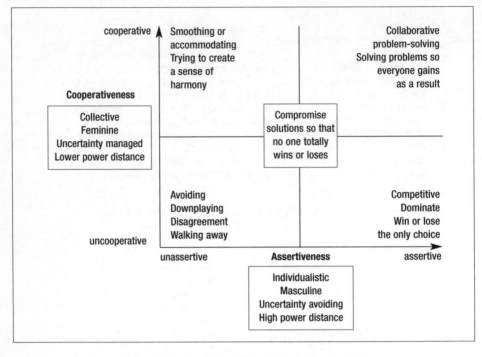

Figure 9.11 Conflict handling on international projects
Source: Law (1998)

classic measurements of time, cost and quality will, of course, prevail. But the project manager also needs to consider behavioural factors which will impact on the hard 'output' measures.

From her study on a Malaysian project, Law (1998) drew up a framework for managing multicultural projects based upon the relationship between the degree of multiculturalism and project complexity. She suggests that the project management focus must shift its emphasis according to the level of multiculturalism among team members and stakeholders, and needs to take into account the complexity of the project (Figure 9.12). Multiculturalism means the numbers and types of different nationalities. Complexity refers to size, technical factors and scope. According to these variables the project management focus will change.

PARADIGM SHIFT

Increasingly, corporations that are striving to exploit the opportunities of world markets are reconfiguring their structures and changing the mental mindset of

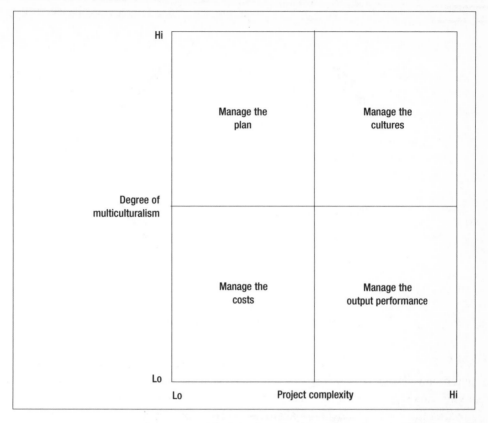

Figure 9.12 Managing multicultural projects
Source: Adapted from Law (1998)

the enterprise to help them deliver benefits of cultural diversity. Bartlett and Ghoshal (1989) proposed the Transnational Organizational Model as one which international corporations will aspire to achieve. Their conclusions suggest that global efficiencies have to be accompanied by local responsiveness and organizations should see diverse resources and diverse capabilities as strengths rather than obstacles to achieving success. Mechanisms for sharing information and sharing learning have to be put in place so that the potential advantages of diversity are realized.

For domestic-focused businesses the attainment of such an organizational model requires a paradigm shift, which for many will be revolutionary. Some profoundly held attitudes and behaviours will need to change. The belief cycle example in Figure 9.13 suggests commonly held beliefs in many UK organizations that will be under severe pressure to change. These types of beliefs may be built on hundreds – even thousands – of years of 'doing things a certain

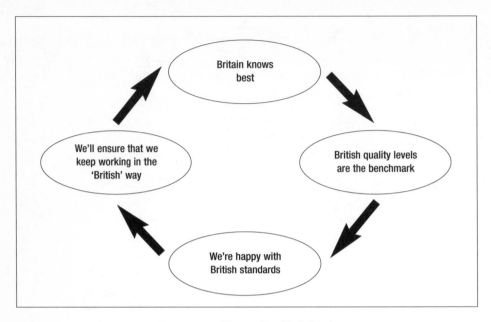

Figure 9.13   Mono-cultural belief cycle
© Cultural Fluency Training and Development Ltd 2000

way'. For neutral observers the resultant behaviours may be described as potentially arrogant, possibly based upon technical superiority which disappeared a long time ago. One of the tasks for senior executives driving their businesses towards the idea of 'transnationalism' is to break into these cycles to leverage the advantages of cultural diversity. As a first step, an understanding of the links between beliefs, values, attitudes and behaviours is needed. If we align the beliefs with the bedrock elements of culture we can then see how emergent value and attitude sets will influence the development of work and management systems. Finally, the behaviours that physically and mentally touch us break the surface. Figure 9.14 models the links between beliefs, values, attitudes and behaviours as a cross-cultural comparison.

Some organizations have woken up to advantages of transnationalism but the majority have not yet climbed onto the starting blocks. Organization development efforts are increasingly likely to be ever more aligned with the need to manage transcultural change – change across national cultures. This represents a huge challenge for which most corporations are ill-prepared. Evidence from the field suggests this will be a long process, probably far longer than standard change management programmes in mono/domestic cultural environments. In fact, players in many industries worldwide have little choice but to climb aboard. The smart companies are starting to make that journey now.

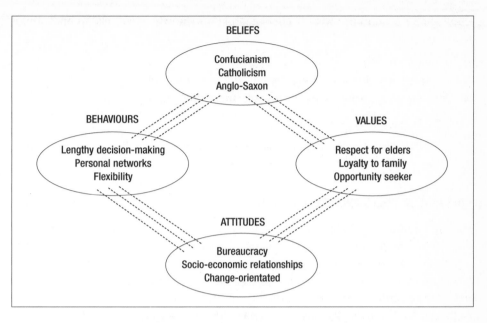

Figure 9.14   Cross-cultural behaviour/belief cycle
© Cultural Fluency Training and Development Ltd 2000

What are some of the outcomes of such developments? There are several:

1. The national identity of the corporation may become quite diluted, heavily and deliberately so in some instances as organizations see marketing benefits from these developments. Telecommunications, power-generation and airlines are good examples of industries where this has started to happen.
2. Human resource strategies will need to be rethought. What type of people will organizations operating in transnational marketplaces be looking for? What key skills and competencies will be sought? Where should companies pitch their recruitment initiatives? And, of course, how should projects be resourced and managed?
3. Product innovation can be significantly improved through cultural 'recontextualization', enabling more effective differentiation to be achieved.
4. Challenging the way things are done in a particular culture can lead to process improvement, creativity and innovation in project working.

CULTURAL FLUENCY

One of the key features to emerge from these developments is the concept of the culturally fluent organization. The ability of companies to achieve transcultural success is increasingly dependent upon a genuine understanding of how people

153

do business around the world. This capability is known as cultural fluency and is achieved through:

- gaining an awareness of cultural norms
- acquiring specific knowledge of cultural environments
- developing relevant skills for transcultural working.

Cultural fluency may be defined as:

> The repertoire of cross-cultural awareness, knowledge and skills needed by people to perform effectively across international territories.

CULTURAL TRAINING AND DEVELOPMENT

Clearly, cultural fluency implies that specific training and development programmes need to be initiated to help people achieve appropriate levels of competency. The aggregate of these skills and competencies across the organization, the transformation of structures, processes and procedures, and the change of mindset from mono-culturalism to multiculturalism identifies the culturally fluent organization. Traditionally, businesses have seen the performance of their people in foreign markets linked to their ability to communicate in different languages. Languages are important, but language fluency is no longer the sole criteria for success in these environments. Global marketplaces have intensified, each diverse customer base having its own language. This drives the need for a lingua franca such as English. People are moving between cultures with greater frequency as they work on global assignments. It is unrealistic to expect language fluency in a short time. As global environments change so too must training and development responses. Solutions should be built on a clear identification of needs. When these are fully understood, appropriate programmes can be targeted for the right audience. Language fluency is one potential training solution but now a range of cost-effective approaches and programmes are available to organizations. Figure 9.15 shows the process for the formulation of appropriate training and development responses.

1. *Strategic cultural fluency* These roles involve strategic relationships across cultures – international business development, alliances and partnerships. Effective management of these relationships calls for special awareness of cultural behaviour at a senior level.
2. *Workgroup cultural fluency* Leading multicultural teams and international projects requires a repertoire of skills and techniques. The life span of global teams may be short, demanding excellence in team formation, development and close-out. Project managers need to acquire dexterity in managing multicultural stakeholders.

3. *Personal cultural fluency* Individual performance in handling working relationships and social etiquette can be enhanced through the acquisition of specific skills and knowledge. Interpersonal behaviour can be improved through foreign language learning, international English training and non-verbal communication skills.

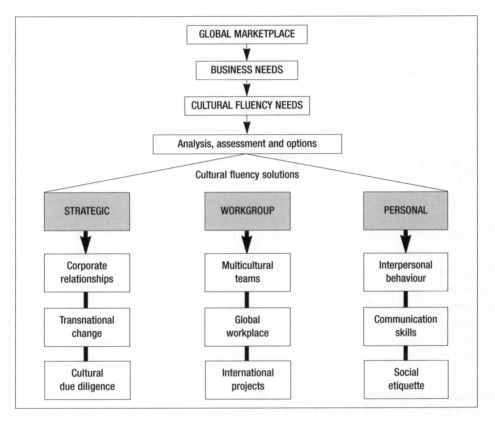

Figure 9.15   Cultural training and development planning
© Cultural Fluency Training and Development Ltd 2000

For large projects, training programmes may be required to help manage cultural diversity between stakeholders. The model in Figure 9.16 can be applied to any cultural situation.

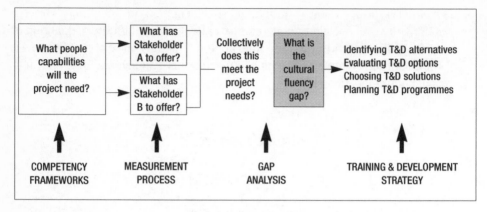

Figure 9.16   Transcultural projects – training and development strategy formulation
© Cultural Fluency Training and Development Ltd 2000

CONCLUSIONS

Culture is a word which produces a complexity of meanings, interpretations and concepts. If we accept that culture influences how projects are implemented and what is achieved then we must understand what elements shape a culture and its associated cultural behaviours. Therefore, project managers will need to pay increasing attention to managing culture effectively. This means managing cultural diversity within the project itself, understanding the cultural environment in which the project operates and striking a balance between cultural, technical and operational factors. Particularly when the international and cross-border dimensions of projects are considered, the management of culture is perhaps one of the greatest challenges facing project managers in today's global business environment.

REFERENCES AND FURTHER READING

Bartlett, C. and Ghoshal, S. (1989), *Managing Across Borders: The Transnational Solution*, HBR Press, Boston, MA.

Garrison, T. (1998), *International Culture*, 2nd edition, Elm Publications, Huntingdon.

Handy, C. (1985), *Understanding Organisations*, 3rd edition, Penguin, London.

Harbison, J. and Pekar, P. (1998), *Smart Alliances*, Jossey-Bass, San Francisco.

Hofstede, G. (1994), *Cultures and Organisations*, Harper Collins, London.

IPD (1998), *Issues in People Management No 22*, Institute of Personnel and Development, London.

Law, J. (1998), 'An investigation of national cultural factors impacting the management of an international project in South East Asia', unpublished MBA dissertation, Henley Management College.

Mole, J. (1995), *Mind Your Manners*, Nicholas Brealey, London.

Morsing, M. (ed.) (1998), *Managing the Unmanageable for a Decade*, Oticon, Copenhagen.

Swierczek, F. W. (1994), 'Culture and conflict in joint ventures in Asia', *International Journal of Project Management*, **12**(1).

Trompenaars, F. (1993), *Riding the Waves of Culture*, Economist Books, London.

Trompenaars, F. and Hampden-Turner, C. (1997), *Riding the Waves of Culture*, 2nd edition, Nicholas Brealey, London.

Turner, J. R. (1999), *The Handbook of Project-based Management*, 2nd edition, McGraw-Hill, London.

10 Managing ethics

Alistair Godbold

Interest in business ethics has grown in reaction to well-publicized scandals, including the fraud-related collapse of former 'blue chip' companies such as Polly Peck, Ferranti, Maxwell Communications, ENRON and World Com, the dirty tricks campaign by British Airways against Virgin Atlantic, and the allegations of insider dealing in Blue Arrow by County NatWest. In America Sears Roebuck & Co. came under fire for its dubious car repair services. The list continues with companies such as General Dynamics, Daniels-Midland Co., NYNEX Columbia/HCA Healthcare Corp., Guinness and BCCI. All of these companies lost money as a result of their unethical actions and in some cases went out of business altogether. The above are the infamous and the large scale, there are many more that impact on a local scale or have yet to come to public notoriety. On the other hand, it is important when considering ethics in business, and more specifically in project management, not to become puritanical, and to remember that you are in business. The aims of the business, or a project, are not somehow rendered more profound or acceptable by attaching to them a spurious social or philosophical dimension. All that achieves is to remove the clarity that ensures that people do what is right in business and projects. Business and projects must be seen and managed in the wider context of all of the stakeholders, not just the narrow pursuit of a commercial aim, cost and timescale.

The ethical content of an organization's actions is only significant when there is a transaction with a stakeholder. Where there is no such transaction, there is no basis to judge the ethical content of an action. Business today is becoming more complex and more interrelated with other social phenomena. It is also international, operating in a world of complex social and economic interdependencies. Pressure groups are becoming more powerful, exercising legitimate power and representing the views of large sections of society. This was the case when Greenpeace mounted a campaign against Shell's plans to sink the Brent Spar oil platform in the North Atlantic. The actions of the company came under public scrutiny through the interests of the pressure groups, the media, the general public and Parliament.

In the opening paragraph I recalled some of the more obvious ethical issues, those that 'the man on the Clapham omnibus' would recognize as being an ethical decision. However, there are many more decisions in our everyday management careers that individually may be considered a matter of style, but when taken together project an image of how we behave, ethically or unethically.

The ethical dilemmas are those everyone can recognize, insider share dealing, accepting or offering bribes, and so on. However, today's business and projects are composed of relationships with stakeholders, employees, members of the project team, customers, suppliers, users and people affected by the secondary impact of any change process. These are not one-time relationships; we may have to continue doing business with these people as customers, suppliers or partners in the future. In the short term it can pay to be unethical, you may win the contract by spotting a loophole in the specification, and choose to exploit it, you may improve your cash flow by paying your suppliers late or gain prestige by taking credit for the actions of a subordinate. These are all short-term advantages paid for by loss of long-term gains. The company's, or individual's, reputation in the marketplace precedes it and there are a finite number of players in any market. If we do not have a successful relationship with any of them, it may affect the competitive position of the company and the flexibility that any stakeholder is prepared to accept in this relationship. Business is about people, the relationships that people in business have with each other and the way in which they interact. Projects are a micro-environment of these relationships: project manager to team, project to customer, to user, and so on. The management of these relationships is vital to the continuing success of the project or the parties taking part in them.

For the majority of people, working under pressure of deadlines and budgets, these relationship issues need to be actively managed. However, this chance of short-term gain through unethical behaviour is likely to occur frequently. The ability to recognize it, and resist its attractiveness, is that much more difficult. The principles for managing this kind of issue are similar to those needed to manage 'ethical dilemmas'. The application of these principles needs to be considered on a smaller scale than that described here.

ETHICS AND PROJECT MANAGEMENT

A project is an activity different from the steady state of an organization. Projects may be undertaken by companies with temporary teams to achieve a set task, by groups who will work on one project, then move on to work on the next, or companies that specialize in projects for clients. All of these temporary teams have to work with each other and with other companies whom they may not have dealt with before. To establish a relationship quickly and start to work together it is important that there is a cultural fit between the two companies, that they can do business together.

The traditional view of the role of the manager is, as Milton Friedman (1970) put it, 'to make as much money as possible while conforming to the basic rules of society'. This principle can be applied to project managers as their role is to get the project completed on time and to budget, legally. This narrow definition is dysfunctional as it denies acknowledgement of the role other people play in fulfilling the objective of the project. A project cannot succeed without the help of senior management, the project team, suppliers, users and the customer. The above definition of project management implies a style of 'I win you lose', whereas projects are a non-zero sum game, both parties have to gain. Recognizing this interdependence under the pressure of deadlines and budgets requires a developed skill or judgement of the manager, except under the most obvious circumstances, and the pursuit of the long-term goal.

Projects are agents of change, they upset the status quo, and as such they can expect to meet resistance. Not only do projects create change in the organization as their principal product, they create change by the process in which they go about it. They are unique and as no norms have been established for them, this in itself may create uncertainty within their own structure. Projects use a variety of resources to achieve their objectives and these need to be integrated. They also produce change not only for the end-users of the change (building, computer system, business process, office move, and so on) but also for those people involved in getting to this end state. During these times of change people may feel insecure or threatened by the alteration of the status quo. These people will need to be able to trust the honour and openness of the project in order to contribute to its success. If they feel that the project has some hidden threatening agenda, this will add one more reason to resist the change brought about by the project. This is not to say that the outcome of the project must be of benefit to all, but that they must be clear and sensitively handled. If the outcome of the project is to reduce staff numbers, then this must be clearly articulated and people kept informed at every stage of the process. In order to reduce the risk to a project, it must be seen as ethical and trustworthy. For the project manager, discrete moral leadership rather than a public relations exercise is the key to reaping the benefits of ethics for temporary projects, individual project managers and the organizations for the long term.

This constant change and instability is one of the factors that differentiate the management of projects from the management of operations. Projects do not have a stable background against which to build up norms of behaviour and procedures. Instead, these norms and procedures have to be built up in a very short time in a very dynamic environment. A side effect of this is that there is no time to adapt and evolve these procedures as by the time they have been tried the environment has moved on. As a consequence project managers have a high degree of control over the health, welfare and well-being of all their stakeholders including team members. Another problem for project managers is that the members of their teams, customers and users will have their own different sense of morality, coming as they do from different backgrounds. This means project managers must clarify the values of the whole group to prevent any adverse clash of values in their relationships.

One of the duties of a project manager is to balance competing objectives of quality, cost, time and scope. Each of the project stakeholders – co-contractors, the project director, team members, the functional organization, subcontractors, users and society – has expectations of how these objectives will be balanced in accordance with its own perspectives. The relative weights applied to each of these stakeholders and the choices between the generic project goals will vary depending on the type and stage of the project (Mantel and Kloppenborg 1990). In most projects, cost is the most important goal once the specifications are set, and time becomes the most important as the project nears completion. It is this myopic concern with one or two variables that may put the project manager under ethical pressure to disregard the holistic needs of the other stakeholders. In this situation the project manager may manipulate the figures and compromise certain aspects of the project in order to satisfy this small number of variables. The figures may be manipulated or have a different spin put on them to make the project manager look good in this period, in the hope that everything will be all right in the next. Many managers see this practice as not too unethical due to the intense pressure they are under to perform (Bruns and Merchant 1990).

Project managers are leaders, they have views and beliefs shaped by their background, education and experiences. They, as managers, must pervade all operations throughout the project. They therefore have a key responsibility to manage the values of the project to ensure that they are effective in every action and that the agendas of the many stakeholder groups are balanced and 'ethical'. The project manager must manage the project with a set of values congruent with those of society and the stakeholders, and it is his or her responsibility to ensure that a common set of values are communicated throughout the life of the project. This is not only the responsibility of the project manager; project team members have a duty to themselves to ensure that their own work matches these values. Unless the project manager is aware of all of these relationships and responsibilities he or she will not be providing the optimum base for the project.

There are many aspects of the project manager's role that influence how ethically the manager performs the job, and how responsible he or she feels for the actions of the team. A major problem is the amount of information generated about progress, finance, decisions, views of stakeholders, and so on. If this information is all passed to the project manager then he or she will suffer from 'information overload' and a large amount of the information passed to the project manager may be lost, degrading the manager's performance. Therefore it is important that the project manager receives only relevant information. However, this relies on a hierarchy of team leaders and work package managers deciding what is relevant and filtering the information. This filtering can introduce a bias of successive levels of management removing information that shows them in a bad light or is in their opinion not relevant, leading to 'negative information blockage'. This bias, or blockage, may not allow the project manager to manage because he or she does not have all the relevant information. Perhaps more importantly, the blockage will allow the middle levels of management to cover up bad or unethical practice. This might occur because they are trying to make themselves look good, but a more common problem is the emotional attachment they feel to a project. As people work on a project they become more committed to it and begin to feel any obstacle can be overcome and this may prevent them from recognizing real problems. It is the leader's role to ensure that channels of communication are open to allow all team members access to the project manager to report any issues that give them cause for concern, so that the manager does not have to rely totally on the information filtering through the hierarchy.

The most serious problem in terms of the pressure put upon the project manager lies perhaps in the role's most basic function: the interface between management and the professional discipline. Normally a project manager is expected to have a high level of skill in the field in which the project is conducted; in most engineering projects this will involve the project manager being an engineer. An engineer deals with the facts of the profession, designs, calculations and the more abstract notion of engineering judgement. The engineer's role is to assemble data and perform calculations to determine the course of action. A manager coordinates resources and takes decisions based on the recommendations of the team. However, the project manager is at the interface of these two roles; he or she must not only take decisions, but take them based on 'professional judgement'. In normal circumstances the distinction between the two roles can be maintained. However, when under pressure this distinction, with its associated moral and ethical consequences, can break down.

This section has shown the pressures and complications that are brought together in the role of project manager. The project manager has a great responsibility to the team, the public, the company and all other stakeholder groups. As a result of this the scope and nature of the job make it a very demanding but rewarding role.

ETHICS AS A DIFFERENTIATOR

Much has been written in the press, the media and in everyday business dealings about the detrimental effect of ethics on business. However, ethics can be used as a positive differentiator. By differentiating itself from the competition, a company may be able to gain advantage. Ethics and competition are not mutually exclusive; competition is an essential part of business. Once equality in cost of production is achieved in a market, or cost of execution of a project, then the only way to stay in business is to become more efficient or differentiate. Many companies are already competing on these grounds, for example ethical investment funds, producers of green products and firms that trade on their ethical image.

In any business or project a company can possess three competitive weapons (Garvind 1992): productivity, quality and new products. Ethics can be added as a fourth weapon. To realize this edge, leadership, innovation and communication are needed. All of these are qualities of the good manager, and essential qualities of the project manager. In managing the ethics of a group, there are many parallels between ethics and quality. Both embody the long-term perspective, are customer-led, and involve doing things right and doing the right things. Where organizations have adopted and internalized a strong ethical culture that they can sustain, they are able to exploit this as a competitive advantage. The organization's reputation with its customers, employees and even suppliers of some high value added products can build strong relationships and lasting confidence. This can act as a barrier to entry to new firms entering the market. This tactic must be used with care as stakeholders and observers will look for lapses from this policy which may be harmful to the project. These lapses may be exploited by competitors or those who have some other agenda for the project and do not wish to see it achieve some of its outcomes.

ETHICAL THEORY

To discuss the role that ethics play in project management it is necessary to present ethical points in terms of the underlying ethical theory. This section illustrates why it is important to understand this theory not only for use in this discussion, but for managers to think about and present their ethical arguments.

To argue the case of a moral viewpoint, managers need to be able to articulate these arguments in a form that is intellectually and theoretically valid. Some authors argue that, in addition to the skills of ethical analysis and reasoning, ethical enquiry often requires an understanding of the nature of basic ethical principles, the status of knowledge in ethics and the relationships among ethics, law and religion (Benjamin and Curtis 1981). In many cases the moral values of managers, project managers and executives may often conflict with their role duties. What, according to Gandz and Hayes (1988), managers and executives are deficient in, are the skills of ethical analysis which allow them to reconcile their roles as managers and as socially integrated individuals. Not only must the managers be able to argue an ethical position in coherent terms, but they must be able to articulate this view to their peers and the various stakeholders in the company, or in the case of a project manager, the project. As Solomon (1985) puts it:

> No competent executive would think of taking the company to the bargaining table without a clear sense of objectives, limits and tactics. And yet some of the same executives lead their companies into the forum of public opinion with nothing but a grab bag of ethical platitudes.

The traditional way of reducing the variety of values, whether ethical or not, is to seek general principles. The principles or theory try to avoid the arbitrary treatment of individuals and cases and allow for consistency in policy and judgements. To be able to reason, articulate and discuss ethical issues, it is important to understand some basic philosophical theories in the field of ethics. The following paragraphs give an overview of the main ethical theories. There are two approaches to ethical theory: the rule-based approach and the utilitarian approach. The first says that there are a set of rules you must obey, the second suggests that you should do that which will produce most good.

The central thesis of deontological ethics (rule-based) is that the consequences of actions are not the primary consideration in deciding what ought to be done (Bowie and Duska 1990); it is the consideration of fairness and justice that takes precedence over the consequences of actions. These rule-based theories can be broken down into two types: absolute and conditional theories. The absolute theories, the main one of which is Kant's categorical imperative, say that people must do certain things if they are to be morally right. The conditional theories, such as prima-facie duties, also advocate a set of rules but suggest how and when it is appropriate to modify these duties.

The categorical imperative form of ethics was developed by Immanuel Kant (1724–1804). He attempted to show that there are certain moral rights and duties that all humans must follow, regardless of the benefits or otherwise that the exercising of these rights will accrue to the individual or to others (Velasquez 1992). This theory assumes that everyone should be treated as a free person

165

equal to everyone else. Everyone has a right to such treatment and everyone must treat others in this way. The essence of the categorical imperative lies in the three criteria for moral correctness:

1. *Universality* The individual's reasons for acting must be reasons that everyone could act on, at least in principle.
2. *Transitivity* The person's reasons for acting must be reasons that he or she would be willing to have all others use as a basis of how they treat him or her.
3. *Individuality* The person 'should treat each human being as a person whose existence as a free rational person should be promoted' (Gandz and Hayes 1988).

The conditional rule-based ethics from the utilitarian aspect can be summarized in these two principles (Velasquez 1992):

1. An action is right from an ethical point of view if, and only if, the action would be required by those moral rules that are correct.
2. A moral rule is correct if, and only if, the sum total of the utilities produced if everyone were to follow that rule is greater than the sum total utilities produced if everyone were to follow some alternative rule.

In the rule-utilitarian approach, the fact that a certain action would maximize utility does not make it moral. In this approach you must first find the correct rule and then apply the utility criterion. The most common form of conditional rule-based approach from the adaptation of rule-based ethics is prima-facie duties. A prima-facie rule takes the form that other things being equal, one should tell the truth, obey the law and so on. The theory states that there are prima-facie (at first sight) duties that are morally binding and that ethical decisions constitute deciding which is the more obligatory, if and when there is a conflict. The six prima-facie duties are (Gandz and Hayes 1988):

- fidelity
- gratitude
- justice
- beneficence (the act of doing good)
- self improvement and
- non-maleficence.

The main problem with this theory is determining which is the appropriate rule, causing the user to focus too narrowly on the means, rather than the ends. Another problem is when duties conflict, deciding what weight and merit should be applied to each. Some argue this form can degenerate into traditional utilitarianism, by allowing the rules that give beneficial expectations more utility than those that do not allow such expectations (Velasquez 1992).

There are a number of ethical theories that explicitly designate some intrinsic aspect of the human act as the criterion for moral goodness or badness. Hedonism is an example of one of these forms of ethics. Its roots can be traced back to ancient Greece. The theory holds that as long as an act is capable of producing some pleasure (*Hedone* in Greek), it is good. This form of ethics has evolved to emphasize more rational pleasures and the promotion of peace of mind. Utilitarian ethics is a development of this theory. The theory is variously known as best result ethics, egoism or end point ethics (Gandz and Hayes 1988). The main exponents of this theory were Jeremy Bentham (1748–1832), and John Stuart Mill (1806–73). The essence of the theory can be stated as:

> An action is right from an ethical point of view if and only if the sum total of the utilities produced by the act is greater than the sum total of the utilities produced by any other act.
>
> (Velasquez 1992)

This form of ethics, it is argued, will naturally lead to a division of labour that will produce the best outcome for society (Bowie and Duska 1990). Thus, if people take responsibility for their own roles, society will flourish. However, there are many problems with this approach to ethics. For example, how does one estimate the plurality of values, happiness, pleasure, health, knowledge, friendship, comfort, pain, harm, and so on, to evaluate the consequences of a proposed course of action? Even if one can estimate the utility of an action, you cannot simply add and subtract the various positive and negative consequences of the alternative courses of action. Further problems arise with this theory, mainly due to the concept of justice.

The relativist theory is perhaps the most contentious theory of all those discussed so far. It has become most fashionable since the Second World War. In its clearest form it is based on the existentialist philosophy of Jean-Paul Sartre. The essence of this argument is that ethics are merely a matter of taste (Donaldson 1992), and if one culture or country prefers one set of rules there is little that can be said or done about it. Sartre argued that there is a basic human nature given to us by a great designer, God, and so nothing to bind us by a certain way of action (Varga 1980). In this form of ethics, what people make of themselves stems from their own free actions, they create their values depending on their own situations and circumstances. These sentiments can be summarized by the expression, 'When in Rome it's all right to do as the (good) Romans do.'

Relativism avoids any attempt at paternalism and does not impose universal moral standards. This can be used to justify bribing foreign officials in order to gain a contract. If this is the accepted practice in the host country but not in the home country of the competing firm, it is still ethical to indulge in this practice. This form of action can be extended to environmental contamination and low levels of safety for workers which are acceptable in the society in which the projects are undertaken. There are many arguments against this form of ethics. Bernard Williams in his book *Morality* (1972) describes relativism as 'the anthropologist's heresy, possibly the most absurd view to have been advanced in moral philosophy'. Others have argued that if this theory were accepted without any restrictions, no order could be maintained in society and no state could function (Varga 1980). These objections forced even Sartre to modify the theory to a more acceptable form.

ETHICS ABROAD

Many project companies now compete nationally and internationally. Many are global, with infrastructures or centres of expertise shared across national boundaries. When companies and their staff operate in this environment, problems can, and do, occur. They lose the backdrop of shared attitudes, familiar laws, judicial procedures and standards of ethical conduct. Practices that worked in the home country may not work in the host country. There may be different ethical conduct or cultural norms. This is not to say that one set of standards is better than another or that companies must abide by the higher standard in both of the moral codes. Some ethical theories, such as relativism, suggest that there is no absolute measure of ethical standards, just statements of the fashion of society at the time. I have heard of examples of companies that have sent engineers to work on projects abroad but have had to recall them due to their inability to reconcile their own ethical standards, congruent with their home country, with those of the country in which they find themselves working. This causes problems not only for the individuals and their perception of their career, but for the company in how to manage and resource the project. A way of resolving this is to use cultural relativism.

Problems involved when projects are conducted in multicultural environments with no reference points are many and not easy to resolve. However, the rest of this section provides some guidance on how practices that are just different may be distinguished from those that are wrong. Some cultures place different emphasis on equally valid ethical codes which may cause confusion. Americans place greater emphasis on liberty than loyalty, whilst the Japanese place emphasis on loyalty to their company and business networks. These issues may be addressed explicitly up front, before staff are exposed to these dilemmas. By giving staff a framework in which to think about these issues, they will be better equipped to deal with the issues for the benefit of themselves, the company and the project on which they are employed. When shaping the ethical behaviour of staff, or a company based in a foreign culture, you must be guided by three principles (Donaldson 1996):

- respect for core human values, which determine the absolute threshold for all business activities
- respect for local traditions
- the belief that context matters when deciding what is right and what is wrong.

In Japan the giving and receiving of gifts is an integral part of business life. Many western cultures may consider this custom as not just different, but wrong, as it could be seen as trying to unduly influence someone (bribery). Many companies have come to respect this tradition and have different limits for the giving and receiving of gifts in Japan than they do in the rest of the world. Respecting local traditions also means recognizing the strengths and weaknesses of different ethical norms. In the Far East, stealing credit from a subordinate is nearly an unpardonable sin.

The phenomenon of globalization in business suggests that for the world to be ethical and just there must be some global ethic. There are international regulatory frameworks and laws, and courts are emerging to deal with the technical issues of globalization, but the global business ethic is not yet here to help the project manager. But there have been many events contributing towards the creation of a global ethic (Kung 1997). The basic principles of the emerging global ethic are as follows:

1. Justice: just fair conduct, fairness, exercise of authority in maintenance of right.
2. Mutual Respect: love and respect for others.
3. Stewardship: human beings are only the stewards of natural resources.
4. Honesty: truthfulness and reliability in all human relationships (integrity).

These principles are more abstract than those contained in a company or professional institution ethics statement, but they do provide a mental framework in which to address these issues at a macro level.

PRACTICAL HELP

Throughout this chapter I have discussed the role of ethics in management and more specifically project management, the role of ethics in the long-term view, the background to ethical theory and the specifics of managing ethics in a global business or at least a project in a foreign country. However, there are times when the manager does not have the luxury to think about the philosophical dimensions of an ethical dilemma and this is where a more prescriptive checklist or rule of thumb can be of use. The rules of thumb for ethical decision-making (in the domestic setting) come in varying degrees of complexity, some more useful than others. A more comprehensive rule that provides a mental framework in which to draw out many of the issues in a decision is described below (Dreilinger 1994):

1. Which *goals* or *priorities* does this solution support or work against?
2. Does the solution reflect the *values* of the organization and the decision-makers?
3. What are the *consequences* (in terms of benefit or harm) and ramifications (effect of time and outside influences) for each of the stakeholders in the following three areas: cost-to-benefit, rights-to-equity and duties-to-obligation? Are there any other consequences?
4. What qualms would the decision-maker have about the *disclosure* of a favourable decision to this solution to the CEO, board of directors, family, the public?
5. What is the positive or negative *symbolic potential* of this solution if understood – or misunderstood – by others? Will it contribute to building and maintaining an ethical environment?

Whenever making a decision that has some ethical dimension, it is important to keep monitoring the outcomes of the decision at every stage. This ensures that the decision is still the best and that any corrective action can be identified early.

CONCLUSIONS

In this chapter I have discussed how ethics play an increasingly important role in business. This is due to many factors, including the heightened awareness of workers and the general public, and as a reaction against the greed and avarice of the 1980s. All managers, especially project managers, are under pressure to take short cuts, improve the figures and get immediate results. This puts them under ethical pressure. The decisions that the project manager takes are much less restricted than those in line management. The result of this is that project managers operate in a relatively unbounded, dynamic, often international environment, giving them greater freedom and scope, and their decisions wider effect. A more serious characteristic of project management, putting project managers under more ethical pressure, is the weak distinction between their professional and managerial roles. The international nature of many projects brings with it its own special set of ethical problems that must be handled for both the team members involved in the project and the project manager executing the project. To help the project manager deal with these ethical pressures there needs to be a more structured framework in which to take decisions.

A point made in this chapter is that much of today's management and especially project management is conducted in a complex interrelated environment with a finite number of players. If project managers are to succeed in this environment, they must be aware of these interrelationships and the impact they can have on the success of the project, or their next project and their career.

Ethics in projects and business need not be a threat but an opportunity, a way of differentiating yourself from the competition and exploiting some form of competitive advantage. This differentiation is best handled subtly and not as a public relations exercise. It can bring lasting benefits which may not only attract new business, but also ease the path to the completion of projects.

In this chapter several methods have been outlined that will assist project managers in their duties. These include an understanding of the background of ethical theory, an understanding of the issues that may face project managers, the way in which ethics play a vital role in the success of a project, both from the ethical dilemma and from the relationship maintenance perspective. A rule of thumb has been provided to act as a first check to help project managers consider the issues involved. Where projects are conducted in an international environment a further framework has been included to help the manager also assess and resolve these issues.

REFERENCES AND FURTHER READING

Benjamin, M. and Curtis, J. (1981), *Ethics in Nursing*, Oxford University Press, Oxford.

Bowie, N. E., and Duska, R. F. (1990), *Business Ethics*, 2nd edition, Prentice-Hall International, Englewood Cliffs, NJ.

Bruns, W. J. Jr. and Merchant, K. A. (1990), 'The dangerous morality of managing earnings', *Management Accounting*, August.

Donaldson, J. (1992), *Business Ethics: A European Case Book*, Academic Press, London.

Donaldson, T. (1996), 'Values in tension: ethics away from home', *Harvard Business Review*, September–October.

Dreilinger, C. (1994), 'Ethics, what about thou shalt?', *Journal of Business Strategy*, July–August.

Friedman, M. (1970), 'The social responsibility of business is to increase profits', *New York Times Magazine*, 13 September.

Gandz, J. and Hayes, N. (1988), 'Teaching business ethics', *Journal of Business Ethics*, **7**.

Garvind, D. A. (1992), *Operations Strategy*, Prentice-Hall, Englewood Cliffs, NJ.

Kung, H. (1997), 'A global ethic in an age of globalisation', *Business Ethics Quarterly*, **7**(3).

Mantel, S. J. and Kloppenborg, T. (1990), 'Trade-offs on projects: they may not be what you think', *Project Management Journal*, **21**(1), March.

Soloman, R. C. and Hanson, K. (1985), *It's Good Business*, Atheneum, New York.

Velasquez, M. G. (1992), *Business Ethics: Concepts and Cases*, 3rd edition, Prentice-Hall International, Englewood Cliffs, NJ.

Varga, A. C. (1980), *The Main Issues in Bioethics*, Paulist Press, New York.

Williams, B. (1972), *Morality: An Introduction to Ethics*, Cambridge University Press, Cambridge.

Index

acquisitions, failure factors 144
assessment
    competence 26–7
    project management competence
        22–4
    model 23
assumptions, project teams 74–5
attribute-based approach *see*
        competency model
Australia
    Institute of Project Management
        20–21
    project management, qualifications
        22
avoidance, conflict management 128–9

behavioural approach, leadership
        88–90
behavioural level, business culture 140
belief cycle
    cross-cultural 152–3
    mono-cultural 151–2
benchmarking
    project management competence
        40–41
    project performance 58

career development

'Competence Model' 7–8
    multiple career strategies 7–8
    project workers 9
    project-based organizations 5–8
    spiral staircase career 6, 51
certification, project manager 54
change, and projects 161–2
change agents, stakeholders as 105–6
charter, project teams 69–74
communication
    project teams 75–6
    stakeholders 110
competence(s)
    assessment 26–7
    components 15
    core
        definition 41
        project management as 41
    definitions 14, 16
    job description 23
    knowledge 15, 18
    personality skills 15, 18
    traditional approach 14–15
    see also competency model;
            competency standards;
            project management
            competence
competency model 15–16

career development 7–8
    project management 17–18
competency standards 16–17
    project management
        levels 17
        organizations 19
        qualifications 20, 21
    terminology 17
    threshold performance 16
conflict
    sources 120–21
    stakeholders 120–21
    see also conflict management
conflict management
    avoidance 128–9
    confrontation 128
    diffusion 128
    example 129–30
    international projects 150
    project management 119–20
    project teams 73–4
    reward/risk factor 122–3
    stakeholders 121–8
confrontation, conflict management
    128
contingency approach, leadership
    90–93
contract labour, project-based
    organizations 4–5
corporate approach, project
    management competence 24–7
country ranking, project management
    149
courses, project management 52–3
critical success factors, project teams
    71
cultural fluency 153–4
    definition 154
    personal 155
    strategic 154

training 154–6
    workgroup 154
culture
    audit, stakeholders 146–8
    belief cycle
        cross-cultural 152–3
        mono-cultural 151–2
    business
        behavioural level 140
        iceberg analogy 137–8, 139–40
        models 137–40
        onion analogy 138–9
    definitions 136
    diversity, project-based
        organizations 150–53
    due diligence 144–6
        audit process 145
    and ethics 168–9
    explicit 138
    implicit 138
    integration 144–7
    international 147–50
    multicultural project management
        149–50, 151
    national, dimensions 148–9
    organizational, IPD study 140–41
    project, Oticon company 142–3
    and project management 141–3
    and stakeholders 136
    symbolism 143
    Triangle Test 145–6
    see also cultural fluency

decision making, project teams 77
Delphi technique 77
diffusion, conflict management 128
due diligence, culture 144–6
    audit process 145
duties, ethics 166

effectiveness, project teams,
    measurement 74, 75
employment security, and HRM 9
employment testing, and HRM 10
engineering construction industry
    (ECI)
    experiential learning 50–53
    project manager, development 51
Ericsson, PROPS 56, 57
ethics
    abroad 168–9
    and culture 168–9
    deontological 165
    as a differentiator 164
    duties 166
    and globalization 169
    hedonism 167
    interest in 159
    issues 159, 160
    Kant's categorical imperative 165–6
    practical considerations 170
    and pressure groups 159–60
    and project management 160–64
    and project managers 162–3
    and quality 164
    relativist theory 167–8
    rule-based 166
    theory 164–8
experiential learning
    cycle 46–7
    distribution 58–60
        centres of excellence 59
        international programmes 59
        intranet 59
        self-support groups 59, 62
    engineering construction industry
        50–3
    project management
        mentoring networks 54
        summary 55–6

project management competence
    46–50
project-based organizations 55–62

failure factors
    acquisitions 144
    mergers 144

gender issues, leadership 93
globalization, and ethics 169
goals
    project teams 70–71
    projects 142
groups, self-support, experiential
        learning 59, 62
growth, project teams 77–8

Handy, Charles, on working life 9
headhunting, project workers 10
hedonism, ethics 167
Human Resource Management
    (HRM)
    employment security 9
    employment testing 10
    project-based organizations 8–10
    and projects 1

iceberg analogy, business culture
    137–8, 139–40
influence strategy, stakeholders 121–8
information, for stakeholders 130–32
information system, project
        management 130–32
Institute of Personnel and
        Development (IPD),
        organizational culture study
        140–41
Institute of Project Management,
        Australia 20–21
intranets, experiential learning 59

job description
  competence 23
  project management 23

Kant, Immanuel, categorical
    imperative 165–6
knowledge
  attenuation 57–8
  competence 15, 18
  distribution, procedures 56–7, 61
  reviews 57–8, 61–2
knowledge-based industries, project
    manager, development 53–4
Kolb's experiential learning cycle
    46–8, 55

leadership
  behavioural approach 88–90
  contingency approach 90–93
  definition 84
  gender issues 93
  and management 83–4
  personal qualities 86–8
  theories 85–96
  trait approach 86–8
  transactional 84, 93–4
  transformational 84, 94
  visionary approach 93–6
lifelong learning, project workers 22

management, and leadership 83–4
maturity models, project management
    36–7, 49–50
measurement, effectiveness, project
    teams 74, 75
mergers, failure factors 144
morale building, project teams 79–80
motivation, project teams 123–5
multiple career strategies 7–8

onion analogy, business culture 138–9
operations, projects, comparison 2
organizations
  project management competence
    benchmarking 40–41
    measurement 36–9
  see also project-based organizations
Oticon company
  'Project 330' 142–3
  project culture 142–3

pairing, project manager development
    53–4
  'Nellies' 53–4
people selection
  aim 3–4
  project-based organizations 3–5
performance goals, project teams
    70–71
personal development, project teams
    78–9
personality skills, competence 15, 18
Peter Principle 8
pressure groups, and ethics 159–60
PRINCE 2 56, 61
procedures, knowledge distribution
    56–7, 61
'Project 330', Oticon company 142–3
project information board, project
    teams 80
project management
  competency model 17–18
  competency standards
    guides 19–20
    levels 17
    organizations 19
    qualifications 21
  conflict management 119–20
  as core competence 41
  country ranking 149

courses 52–3
and culture 141–3
  international 147–50
and ethics 160–64
experiential learning
  mentoring networks 54
  summary 55–6
information system 130–32
job description 23
maturity models 36–7, 49–50
multicultural 149–50, 151
processes 33
  maturity scale 39
qualifications, Australia 22
role fluency 143
threshold competencies 25–6
see also project manager
project management competence
  assessment 22–4
    model 23
  corporate approach 24–7
  definition 34
  organizations
    benchmarking 40–41
    development 41–2, 47–8, 49–50,
      60
    experiential learning 46–50
    maturity models 49–50
    measurement 36–9
    procedures 56–7, 61
    questionnaire 39
    spider's web view 37–8
  project manager 34
  project teams 34, 36
project manager
  certification 54
  development
    engineering construction
      industry 51
    knowledge-based industries 53–4

pairing 53–4
  and ethics 162–3
  key task 66
  project management competence
    34
  project teams 80
  roles 35, 80, 161–4
project teams
  assumptions 74–5
  basics 69, 70
  communication 75–6
  conditions for 69
  conflict management 73–4
  critical success factors 71
  decision making 77
  effectiveness, measurement 74, 75
  expectations 67
  growth 77–8
  high-performance 66
  immediate actions 79–80
  morale building 79–80
  motivation 123–5
  performance goals 70–71
  personal development 78–9
  project information board 80
  project management competence
    34, 36
  qualities 68
  responsibilities 72–3
  roles 72–3
  selection 67–9
  team charter 69–74
  team leader 80
  values 71–2
  vision 76
project workers
  career development 9
  headhunting 10
  lifelong learning 22
  skills needed 8–9

see also project managers
project-based organizations
  career development 5–8
  characteristics 10–11, 31–3
  contract labour 4–5
  and cultural diversity 150–53
  experiential learning 55–62
  people management 8–10
  people selection 3–5
  project management competence,
    development 49–50
  reward systems 6–7
projects
  and change 161–2
  end, reviews 57–8, 61–2
  failures, reasons 45
  goals 142
  hard 105–6
  and HRM 1
  influencing factors 99–100
  international, conflict management
    150
  operations, comparison 2
  performance, benchmarking 58
  purpose, defining 66–7
  resource requirements 103–6,
    131–2
  roles 34
  soft 105–6
  success factors 45, 103
  transcultural, training 155–6
  vision 67
PROPS, Ericsson 56, 57

qualities, project teams 68
quality, and ethics 164

relativist theory, ethics 167–8
resource requirements, projects
  103–6, 131–2

responsibilities, project teams 72–3
reviews, knowledge 57–8, 61–2
reward systems, project-based
    organizations 6–7
reward/risk factor, conflict
    management 122–3
role fluency, project management 143
roles
  project manager 35, 80, 161
  project teams 72–3

SEI Capability Maturity Model 36–7,
  49
selection
  project teams 67–9
  see also people selection
skills, competence 15, 18
spiral staircase career 6, 51
stakeholders
  analysis of 108–12
  as change agents 105–6
  commitment 108–16
  communication 110
  conflict 120–21
    management 121–8
  cultural audit 146–8
  and culture 136
  customers 126–7
  definition 101, 102
  directors 127
  identification 102, 106
  influence strategy 121–8
  information for 130–32
  interests 101
  management
    process 102–16
    strategy 116–17
  register of 106, 107
  satisfaction 100, 101
  senior management 126

success factors, projects 45, 103
symbolism, culture 143

teams *see* project teams
threshold competencies, project
    management 25–6
threshold performance, competency
    standards 16
training
    cultural fluency 154–6
    transcultural projects 155–6
trait approach, leadership 86–8
transactional leadership 84, 93–4

components 94
transformational leadership,
    components 84, 94
Triangle Test, culture 145–6

values, project teams 71–2
vision
    project teams 76
    projects 67
visionary approach, leadership 93–6

working life, Charles Handy on 9

Failsafe IS Project Delivery

Andrew Holmes

With the increasing dependence on information technology, it is vital that organisations deliver their information systems projects effectively. However, it is here where success seems to be as elusive as ever.

Even though IT has become indispensable to almost all of our day-to-day activities, everyone has experience of the problems created by poorly-built IT systems: reduced productivity, increased rework, frustration, and lower customer satisfaction. Success without understanding why has the tendency to breed complacency - a significant risk to any undertaking. Failure, on the other hand, can have the opposite effect - it forces you to learn and provides the opportunity to know how to become more successful. This book looks at how information systems projects can be made more successful, by understanding why and how they fail.

This book lifts the lid on the real reasons why problems with IT persist. It forces organizations to think outside the box - to consider the fundamental reasons why they persistently fail to achieve the success they seek from their information systems projects.

The book is an essential read for decision makers and practitioners alike, especially CEOs, CIOs, IT Directors, IT professionals and business people who have to grapple with the issues presented in this book on a daily basis.

GOWER

The Relationship Manager

The Next Generation of Project Management

Tony Davis and Richard Pharro

Traditionally, project managers have been allocated a project and their role has been to deliver on time, to quality standards and within budget. With hindsight the client only recognises what they really want once the project is delivered – and there is often a gap between expectation and final product. The project management role is now changing and the total impact on the business needs to be addressed more effectively – enter the Relationship Manager.

The true role of the Relationship Manager is to act as an orchestral conductor;

• to go to the client and demonstrate his understanding of the client's short-, medium- and long-term objectives;
• to translate this into a form which the project team can address;
• to receive from the project team a specification of the work to be undertaken, including plans, estimates and schedules, together with detailed work and cost breakdown structures to check that they have really understood what needs to be done and by when – and only when the Relationship Manager is satisfied does he return to the client to sell VALUE.

GOWER

Gower Handbook of Project Management

Third Edition

J. Rodney Turner and Stephen J. Simister

This is a thoroughly revised and restructured edition of the highly successful Gower Handbook of Project Management. The new content is shaped by, and linked to, the body of knowledge produced by the International Project Management Association and the Project Management Institute of the USA, and so will be an invaluable study aid for anyone following either certification programme. In following this framework the book provides comprehensive coverage of the knowledge required both by practising project managers and by those wishing to study the subject.

The book is divided into seven Parts covering:

- The systems of project management
- The context of projects including political, economic, social, technical, legal and environmental issues
- The management of performance including functionality, quality, time, cost, risk and safety
- The management of the project life-cycle
- The management of commercial issues including appraisal and finance
- The management of contracts
- The management of the people involved.

This unique encyclopaedia for the discipline and profession of project management is destined to become a classic that no-one in the field should be without.

GOWER